April 2018

ZORRO
and ME

To Wilma,

Joy & blessings!

Barbara
Dahlgren

Prov. 17:22 "A merry heart is good medicine ... "

ZORRO and ME

Adventures with a Masked Man Wielding a Sword

Barbara Dahlgren

REDEMPTION ◊ PRESS

Published by Redemption Press, PO Box 427, Enumclaw, WA 98022

ISBN 13 (Print): 978-1-63232-099-5
ISBN 13 (eBook): 978-1-63232-100-8
Library of Congress Catalog Card Number: 2009904710

To Those Who've Lived the Journey and
Made the Journey Worth Living:

Zorro (Mel)
Zorro Jr. (Matthew)
The Two Zorrettes (Shelly and Sherisa)

CONTENTS

INTRODUCTION: GOD LOVES TO LAUGH

SOME VIEW GOD as the avenger and picture him sitting on a clouded throne with a scowl on his face. As he points his finger, a lightning bolt shoots forth directed toward people to zap them with a huge electrical shock when they get out of line. When I visualize God, he is here with us, walking beside us. He empathizes when we suffer, he holds us when we cry, and he shares our joy. He weeps with us. He laughs with us.

Does God laugh? I think so. Creating the duck-billed platypus and the giraffe should merit some points on the chuckle meter. Long before animated cartoons desensitized us to talking animals he made Balaam's donkey speak.

The medical profession has come to see what the Bible told us all along: a merry heart is good medicine. Laughter improves emotional, mental, and even physical health. Laughter relieves stress, lowers blood pressure, and strengthens our immune system. Contagious laughter connects us with others. Those who laugh, live longer. God created laughter and it is good.

Of course God has standards. Unfortunately mankind has polluted humor today to something crass and crude, inappropriate, or demeaning to others. God doesn't stoop to such levels. People wouldn't have to lower themselves either, if they learned to laugh at themselves. The ability to see the comical side of everyday life helps one gain perspective and keeps events in context.

Harriet Beecher Stowe once said, "A person without a sense of humor is like a wagon without springs—jolted by every pebble in the road."

What does that mean? Well, it means those who can't see the funny side of life turn the most minor upset into a major offense. They fuss and fume over thwarted plans. They sneer at life's inconveniences. Their defensive attitudes keep them from enjoying daily life.

My ministry is built on this philosophy: God loves to laugh. And if you let him, he will laugh with you. If you don't, he'll laugh at you. I'd rather be laughing with God.

You don't have to wait for someone to tell a joke to giggle. Everyday life is full of humorous possibilities. Our family has learned that lesson through the years, and if we're ever unsure about whether or not something is laughable, we ask ourselves the following four questions:

1. Will this be funny a year from now? Five years from now?
2. Would this be funny if we saw it happening to someone else?
3. Would this be funny if we saw it on a sitcom?
4. Will this be a humorous story we will eventually share with others?

If the answer to any of these questions is "Yes," then we just save ourselves a lot of unnecessary distress and laugh now. We might as well enjoy the ride even though the road is full of pebbles. That's what *Zorro and Me* is all about. This compilation of true stories about our family might help you lighten up and not take yourself too seriously. Remember—God is for us, not against us. And he loves to laugh.

PREFACE

MY NICKNAME FOR my husband of forty years is Zorro. I met Zorro when we were freshmen at a Christian college in Texas. My diary read, "Met Mel Dahlgren today. He's cute but crude and boring." In retrospect I decided he wasn't really crude. He was just an eighteen-year-old boy which can sometimes be synonymous with crude to a seventeen-year-old girl.

By the end of our junior year, Zorro decided he wanted to marry me. I wasn't convinced he was the one for me. I still remember a certain conversation in which he said, "I have just set up a time to counsel about us with the dean of students."

At Christian colleges they like you to counsel about such things. Heaven forbid you marry someone without the powers that be giving their approval—especially if you hope to be used in ministry. Zorro had such a hope.

Hope is about all he had because time and time again he was discouraged from pursuing this desire. He wasn't considered ministry material. Told his voice was too raspy, the faculty dropped him from the public speaking class his senior year—and it didn't help that his face turned bright red every time he spoke in front of the class. He never held any prestigious positions like class president or dorm monitor. He was always the trusty treasurer, sergeant at arms, or assistant to the assistant.

When Zorro told me he was going to counsel about us I tactfully replied, "Let's get something straight. There is a *you* and there is a *me*, but there is *no us*."

Zorro counseled anyway. He was advised not to marry me because he would never be able to control me. Even though he knew it might dash his dream of being a pastor he replied, "I didn't know marriage was about control. I thought it was about love."

I was impressed and yea verily fell in love. There was more to Zorro than met the eye. Then a miracle of miracles occurred. Zorro was hired to be a ministerial trainee in Jacksonville, Florida. So we graduated from college, got married the next day on June 8, 1969, and honeymooned on the way to our first assignment.

That was forty years ago and it's been a wild ride ever since. First impressions can be deceiving because Zorro has been many things but never boring. You'll find that out in this book.

At first glance you may think these stories are intended for pastors and their families. Not true. When God passed out the guardian angel, Zorro got the one with the funny bone. It wouldn't matter if he were a plumber, baker, or candle stick maker. Bizarre things just happen to the guy. The fact that he's in ministry just makes them all the more laughable.

Mel was born in Rhode Island; I in Missouri. We met at college in Texas and have lived in Florida, West Virginia, Kentucky, Washington, Michigan, and California. We even spent ten years in Appalachia. We have three great kids (Shelly, Sherisa, and Matthew) who are all grown and out of the house. Praise God! I love them all dearly, but I think the agony associated with empty nest syndrome was somewhat exaggerated. I now have room for a home office.

Together we have ridden the bumpy road of life. And if you don't think God has a sense of humor and loves to laugh, hold onto your hat and ride along with Zorro and me.

chapter 1

HOW ZORRO GOT HIS NAME

"But know this, that if the goodman of the house had known in what watch the thief would come, he would have watched..."

—Matthew 24:43 (KJV)

WHEN PEOPLE ASK me why I call my husband Zorro I always say, "Well, he looks good in black and carries a sword!" Although that is a fair assessment, I'm going to share with you the true story of how Zorro got his name.

We were working in London at the time. I always love saying that. People "ooooh" and "ahhhhhh." Then I say, "London, Kentucky" and they just stare at me blankly. They would really "ooooooh" and "ahhhhh" if they realized how much we loved the ten years we spent in Appalachia. Our three-church circuit, which took up at least a third of Kentucky, decided to have a costume party for our winter social.

Our dear friends and we made arrangements to leave our young children with a couple who had volunteered to babysit. They lived just off a curvy highway as did almost everyone in the mountainous region. We met our friends there and imagine our surprise when both the guys showed up dressed as Zorro. The costume party was great fun, and after cleanup we headed back to pick up the kiddos. We eased into their long, winding driveway about one in the morning. Because of the cold weather, we left our car running so the kids could get into a warm car. We had just scooped up the children and gone out the door when we noticed our car drifting back down the driveway. Our first thought was, "Oh, no! We forgot to put the emergency brake on."

We braced ourselves for the inevitable crash into a tree but the car seemed to stay on the curving driveway. Suddenly we realized someone was stealing our car. Without hesitation the guys handed us the children, hopped into the other car, and started in hot pursuit of the culprit. Meanwhile, I called the police.

In those days the church leased cars for the ministry and someone had gotten a good deal on these French Peugeots. No one in Kentucky, including us, had ever heard of a Peugeot. You couldn't understand where the lights, wipers, heater, or anything was on the thing without the manual in your hand. Ours, naturally, was a lemon. We took the car to the shop so many times the mechanics started cursing and tried to hide the minute my husband walked through the door.

The car got great gas mileage, though, but you felt like you had to push it up every incline. No matter how many times we had work done on the car, it still made this annoying, clinking clanking sound. To make matters worse we had spilled a gallon, fresh from the cow, of whole milk in it so the smell was a bit overwhelming. Some in the church had affectionately nicknamed it a trashcan on wheels. This poor thief had definitely picked the wrong car to steal.

The conversation with the police started off poorly and went downhill from there.

Me: "Someone has just stolen our Peugeot."

Police: "Your what?

Me: "Our Peugeot!"

Police: "Your poodle?"

Me: "No, no! Our Peugeot! It's our car. It just happened on Highway 190." I just about had them convinced when I blurted out, "And two men dressed up like Zorro are chasing it."

Police: "Sure lady. Call us back when you sober up!" Click.

Meanwhile the two Zorros had chased the Peugeot off the road. When they caught up with the teenage bandit, the windshield wipers were going and the lights were blinking. The poor kid couldn't figure out how anything worked. He hung his head out the window in the below freezing weather and gasped for air because of the smell. I can only imagine what he thought when two masked men in black capes hopped out of the car following him, waved their plastic swords and said, "Unhand that car, you cad!" He was so shocked he stumbled out of the car, tripped, and tumbled down a hill, slamming into the side of a big doghouse. Then he quickly got up and vanished in the moonlight.

The guys had just reached the driveway when they heard the police sirens. As they stopped, the police pulled their guns and shouted into a bullhorn, "Step out of that car!"

Evidently someone at police headquarters had taken me seriously. The two Zorros got out of their cars. After the

3

police stopped laughing, the Zorros gave them a description of the teen, then it was off to the police station to fill out a report. Quite a sight they were, all dressed in black, little plastic swords on their sides, and tiny fake mustaches painted on their upper lips. Things got even funnier when my Zorro had to list his profession as pastor.

We've been to hundreds of church socials over the years but I think this was the most memorable. The teen was caught and, ironically, he was the son of a preacher. When the dad found out Zorro was a minister, he called. "You know how it is in ministry," he said. "You don't have time to spend with your kids."

Yes, we knew. Being in ministry ourselves, we observed how many neglected their families in the name of serving God. The philosophy that if we serve God, he will automatically take care of our families doesn't work. God gave us our families and expects us to nurture and care for them. This incident was a wake-up call for us.

That pastor vowed to spend more time with his son. We promised ourselves we'd spend more time with our children, too. After all, we wouldn't want them to be chased on some moonlit night by two Zorros on mountainous roads in the middle of winter.

Zorro and me at the costume party in Kentucky:
With sword in hand, Zorro is primed and ready to catch the thief.

CHAPTER 2

CATCH A WAVE

"And were beyond measure astonished, saying, He hath done all things well: he maketh both the deaf to hear, and the dumb to speak."

—Mark 7:37 (KJV)

ZORRO AND I graduated from college in Texas in June 1969, got married the next day, and honeymooned on the way to our first ministry assignment in Florida. We drove our old, loaded down '60 Rambler during the day and made love at night. We named our Rambler "Ralph." He had a standard transmission with a roomy front seat so I could sit right next to Zorro. We vowed we would never get a car with a console in the middle because we didn't want to be separated. Oh to be that young and naive again!

Not long after, we had our first disagreement. After the children were born we called them "discussions." To which they'd roll their eyes and say, "Mom and Dad are having a fight."

Of course, they had no idea what a real fight between spouses looked like and I guess we didn't either. However, we've had some strong disagreements and discussions from time to time.

Our first married spat happened on our way to Florida when we stopped for lunch at a little hamburger joint. In the midst of our meal Zorro excitedly said, "Look over there."

I turned my head to see, but there was nothing there. I turned back and Zorro had moved half of my French fries from my plate to his, thinking I wouldn't notice. I was not pleased. I would be eating my French fries in the future and he would eat his.

Zorro and I took turns driving. The second rift occurred because Zorro didn't like the way I was driving. He grimaced as I inadvertently kept sliding the clutch. He could stand it no longer and insisted on driving. We pulled to the side of the road with me in tears and Zorro putting his arms around me saying, "That's all right honey. I like it when you slide the clutch." Aren't young married couples cute?

We alleviated this problem once we got to Florida and bought me a beat-up companion for Ralph. We called her "Rachel." She had an automatic transmission and a console in the middle.

As newlyweds, Zorro and I were adjusting to each other, which is a process we haven't totally mastered after forty years of marriage. Obviously, we had much adjusting to do as we reached Florida, got set up, and Zorro started work as a ministerial trainee. We had to adjust to each other, to living in Florida, to being in ministry, and to the pastor we worked for. Zorro was also adjusting to speaking at church each week. He had been told so many times he would never be used in ministry or be a speaker that he would get physically ill before speaking at church. His name would be announced and he would be in the restroom throwing up, or worse.

I could offer no constructive criticism, only positive reinforcement if Zorro was to have confidence in his speaking ability. Being little miss positive was a stretch for me, but I gave it my all.

We were adjusting to our new schedule, too. Weekends were packed full of church and activities. On weekdays Zorro went with the pastor to visit church brethren or those who had requested visits via our church headquarters.

Ministerial trainees were only to accompany the pastor who did all the visiting and counseling. The pastor Zorro worked for might have been a bit extreme, but Zorro is an easy going, go with the flow type fellow and adjusted to his instructions: never be late, drive the car, don't touch the radio, don't tap your ring on the steering wheel in time to the music, and above all absolutely do not speak during a visit. If any edifying needed to be done, the senior pastor would do it.

Since Zorro was not to speak at all he wanted to at least acknowledge people they met in some way, so he came up with a form of communication he called "the wave." He would raise his right hand about chest high, open the palm toward someone, and slowly move it from side to side. "The wave" was quite versatile. When used slowly with a nod of the head it could mean "hello." When used a little quicker it could mean "goodbye." Zorro had mastered "the wave" by the time they started visiting a man named Bill Dennis.

In those days our custom was to visit someone many, many, many, many times before inviting him or her to church. It doesn't seem logical but in some reverse psychological way it worked. The more we put off asking someone to come to church, the more they were willing to do anything to come. So after the required number of visits,

Bill Dennis was excited to finally be invited to attend our church services. Zorro "waved" goodbye to him as he and the pastor drove away.

Lo and behold the day came when Bill arrived at church. We sang; Zorro gave a mini-sermon before the pastor gave the main message. Immediately after the closing prayer, Bill rushed up to Zorro with arms extended to give him a big bear hug. "I'm so happy. Praise God! My prayers have been answered."

Zorro looked a little perplexed until Bill explained that he had seriously thought Zorro was a deaf mute. From the first time he had met Zorro he had been on his knees praying diligently for God to heal him and let him speak. He thought those prayers had been answered. Zorro almost didn't have the heart to tell him he could speak all along.

The funny thing is I personally think God heard and answered Bill's prayers but not in the way he thought. From that day, forward, Zorro's speaking ability improved greatly. Before, he was a good speaker, but now he had a little something extra, more confidence, and a lot more inspiration. The Lord does work in mysterious ways, which is something I've tried to keep in mind as I travel through life with Zorro. He still waves at everyone he meets. Once you master something you have to use it or lose it.

Our wedding picture: Let the adventures begin!

CHAPTER 3

CAN YOU TOP THAT?

"...the very hairs of your head are all numbered."

—Matthew 10:30 (KJV)

ONE OF THE things I love about Zorro is his lack of vanity. Nevertheless, going bald was a bit of an adjustment for him a few years after we got married. I guess marriage can do that to some people. However, I refuse to take full responsibility. There is that little matter of genetics, you know.

As Zorro glanced at his reflection in the mirror, he decided he needed some advice to help camouflage his condition, so off he went to a new barber in town who specialized in hair styling.

I remember the wisdom of an old Ray Stevens song titled *The Hair Cut* where he admonishes men to always use a barber they are familiar with. If a stranger cuts your hair you could end up looking like one of The Three Stooges.

Unfortunately, we didn't hear that song until after this incident.

The barber said, "Son, I hate to break it to you, but you don't have anything to style. But don't be discouraged. Trust me."

He turned the chair toward him, away from the mirror, and before you could say, "Curly, Moe, or Larry" he shaved what few hairs Zorro had on top of his head, plopped on a toupee, swung the chair toward the mirror and said, "What do you think?"

"I think I want my hair back," Zorro answered.

"Too late for that. Why not try it for a while and see how you like it?"

Why not, indeed? So armed with all sorts of toupee paraphernalia, Zorro headed home. Now, as toupees go, this one looked okay. Bleached by the sun, Zorro's hair had always been more blonde than brown but for the toupee to look natural it had to match the back and sides of his hair, which were brown. It looked a bit unnatural to see Zorro with totally brown hair but c'est la vie.

Then there was that pesky problem of keeping it attached to his head. A friend of ours had little holes poked in his scalp and used special toupee twine to keep his tied down. Although Zorro admired our friend's dedication, he wasn't quite ready to make that kind of commitment. So he opted for special toupee tape, guaranteed to keep the rug firmly affixed to his head. At least that is what the instructions said.

In those days we lived slightly off a curvy, busy two-lane highway in Kentucky. One day Zorro waited for someone he hadn't met before to come to our house to counsel. The man had described his car to Zorro who noticed the guy's car pass by. He hopped in his car to follow the man, stop him and led him back to our house. While standing at this fellow's car on the side of the road, giving him directions, a big semi-truck whizzed past. Imagine this man's surprise as Zorro's toupee flew off and went rolling down the road. The man was in shock but Zorro didn't skip a beat. "Excuse me a minute," he said. "I've got to go chase my hair."

Believe it or not, the man became a church member. This was just one of many toupee incidents. It wasn't so bad for those who knew Zorro wore it, but for the unsuspecting, their astonished expressions were priceless. One time while batting in a baseball game, he swung heartily and saw it land on home plate. He just bent down, dusted off the plate with it and stuck it back on his head. Another time he was playing tag football with the teens and the football skimmed right across his head taking the toupee with it. Then, at the public swimming pool his hair floated off and looked somewhat like a drowning rat. It seemed no amount of super strength toupee tape or glue would hold it. The thought of getting those holes poked through his scalp was too much to fathom.

At church one day Zorro gave a sermon on vanity. To illustrate the point of vanity being a bunch of hot air he blew up a big balloon. Then from the pulpit he let the balloon go. The idea was for the balloon to quickly deflate, but somebody forgot to instruct the balloon. Zorro let the balloon go and it flew out over the top of the congregation. As if in slow motion it circled around and around, here and there, taking its sweet time to deflate. Then as if a magnet drew it to the pulpit again, the last bit of hot air expelled and it landed right on top of Zorro's toupeed head.

Who says God doesn't have a sense of humor? It took awhile for Zorro and the rest of us to stop laughing. Then, as if he planned it, Zorro tied in this mishap to the best sermon on vanity you ever heard.

I'm not sure if this was the catalyst, but not long after that Zorro decided a toupee wasn't for him. Having served him well, the retired toupee is now kept in a shrine in our bedroom drawer, only to come out on special occasions such as costume parties, Dead Rat Day, or when we need a reminder not to take ourselves too seriously. After all, God looks on the heart not the toupee. God has the hairs on our head numbered, and as Zorro always says, "So what if he has a little less to count on mine?"

Zorro wearing his toupee with me, Sherisa, and Shelly:
This is one of the few times it actually stayed on his head.

CHAPTER 4

LEFT BEHIND—
BEFORE IT WAS POPULAR

"Then shall two be in the field; the one shall be taken, and the other left."

—Matthew 24:40 (KJV)

I SMILE WHEN I see the *Left Behind* books by Tim LaHaye and Jerry Jenkins. These popular prophecy-based fiction books trace the drama of those left behind when the Rapture occurs. But long before this series came out, I knew what it was like to truly be *left behind*.

Years ago our annual Ministers' Conference took place in Pasadena, California, instead of the more district-sized ones we hold now. Zorro and I decided it would be more cost effective to drive even though we were living in Kentucky. We could receive mileage reimbursement and use the car to visit friends and family. The kids wouldn't be with us so we could drive straight-through. I slept in the back seat while he drove for three hours or so and then we switched. We were younger then and had more stamina. Now we can barely make it 200 miles without four potty stops and feeling like we need to spend the night in a motel.

Armed with our caffeine drinks, munchies, and trusty CB radio, Zorro drove while I sacked out under a big green blanket in the back seat, until we would switch. This was BC (before cell phones), but CBs were the trend in those days so we skipped the double nickels, put our pedal to the medal, avoided the Smokies, and quipped "10-4 Good Buddy" with the truckers as we zipped down the road. You can check with old CBers or Google to find definitions of those phrases.

The conference was a wonderful combination of all the great f-words: fun, fellowship, friends, family, and food (spiritual and physical). We waved good-bye to California and headed back to Kentucky. About six in the morning, Zorro stopped at a service station in Jackson, Tennessee to get gas. This place wasn't like some of the convenient store gas stations that are popular now. I hazily awoke to see him heading toward the men's restroom. At this one, he needed a key to open the restroom. You've seen them, some keys have something attached to them like a tire, a five-gallon empty can of motor oil, or a two-by-ten block of wood.

It was my turn to drive so I thought I'd save some time and go to the restroom myself. I called to Zorro but, alas, when you finally get the key you don't dilly-dally so he didn't hear me. I grabbed my purse, hopped out of the car, hurried into the women's restroom, did my business, and went back to the car. But the car was gone. I mean like really gone—down the road, out of sight, off and running—gone—and I was literally left behind. As I said before, this was before the age of cell phones and being many, many miles from home, my options were limited.

The guys at the gas station suggested I call the highway patrol and have them put an all points bulletin (APB) out for the car. I thought not. Zorro had a bit of a lead foot in those days and I didn't want him to have a heart attack. I would prefer to kill him myself. Besides, it wouldn't be long before he realized I wasn't asleep in the back seat and he would be right back to get me.

Now when you take turns driving for forty-eight hours or so, you don't really look, feel, or smell your best. Sitting in the gas station listening to the fellas tell each new patron my husband left me behind and people looking in my direction probably thinking, "Yeah, I can see why!" got old. So after about an hour, I decided to get a bite to eat at the Denny's across the street. The guys said they would take any messages for me. Two hours had passed by the time I returned. No word from Zorro yet, so I contented myself with reading a book I bought at Denny's and plotting Zorro's murder. Hell hath no fury like a wife left behind at a gas station.

By now it was around nine. The only store around was a K-Mart up the road a bit so off I trekked to do a little shopping. I charged a bunch of stuff to Zorro's credit card and carried it back to the gas station, making a firm decision that Zorro's death would be a slow one with much suffering. Evidently I had just missed Zorro's phone call to the gas station. I was told not to worry because he was on his way back. I had to wait a couple more hours before he would return so I deposited my shopping bags with the guys who kindly said they'd watch them and I walked back to K-Mart. All right, I thought. I will show mercy. I'll kill him quick so he won't suffer. Maybe I'll run over him with the car in some fit of poetic justice. A jury of my peers (wives) would never convict me. Zorro's perspective was a little different than mine. He had taken his turn driving, filled the car up, went to the restroom, took a quick glance in the back seat and saw the big green blanket I had been sleeping under. "She's sleeping so peacefully," he thought. "I'm feeling really good. I'll let her rest and drive her shift." One hour passed. Two hours passed. About forty-five minutes into the third hour he started getting drowsy. He reached back and said, "Honey," as he tapped the green blanket. "Honey," he said again tapping harder. Then he went into a state of shock as he shouted, "Honey, where are you?"

First he thought I'd fallen out. No, that couldn't happen. Then he thought maybe there was something to this Rapture thing after all. Then, he figured it out. Fortunately he had the gas station receipt with a phone number on it so he found a phone booth and called. He barreled down the road back toward Jackson, talking to other CBers on the road about what had happened. The word kinda got around up and down the highway. One trucker said: "Hey, man! You got a three-hour head start. Why the !@%$#% are you going back? You better keep runnin'."

More than six hours had passed by the time Zorro got back to Jackson. Bill and Charlie (the guys and I were now on a first-name basis) told him he'd find me at K-Mart. When he walked into K-Mart, Sally (the checkout girl and I were also on a first name basis) told him I was looking at puzzles. (Zorro always says I was looking at shoes, but I know I was looking at puzzles. It's amazing how two people can experience the same event and have a different view of what happened. They have a scientific name for this phenomenon. It's called marriage!)

By now I no longer wanted to kill him. You can only keep that kind of momentum going for so long before you pass into some sort of catatonic state.

When I saw him I said, "I really like these two puzzles. Which one should I get?"

He said, "Honey, buy them all!"

And I did. They went nicely with all the other stuff I'd purchased.

Zorro was exhausted so I had to drive the rest of the way home. Someone told us they heard Paul Harvey tell this story on his broadcast the next morning. I don't know if that's true or not, but some of those CB guys Zorro talked to were heading for Chicago which is where Paul Harvey lived and did his broadcast. Back then CBs were a popular form of communication much like the Internet is today.

I do know the Christian journey is like traveling down the highway of life. It's full of twists, turns and unexpected events. Even with all its uncertainties, I'd rather be on the journey than left behind. To assure this, I always announce: "I'm going to the restroom now. And when I get out, this car had better be here waiting for me!"

Zorro and me at the conference in Pasadena, California
before my unfortunate "left behind" adventure

CHAPTER 5

LIFE IS A TRIP

"But my God shall supply all your need according to his riches in glory by Christ Jesus."

—Philippians 4:19 (KJV)

ZORRO WAS SIXTEEN and had just gotten his driver's license and first car, a '56 Nash Ambassador. The car was as big as an ox and just as cumbersome, so he nicknamed her "Oxy."

To christen the vehicle, he and his friend Mitch Knapp planned to take a trip to Canada. They would leave the Los Angeles area, drive up the California coast, stop to see some friends in Oregon, go to Washington, and then over into Canada—an ambitious and exciting excursion for two teen boys in 1963. Keep in mind, there were no super highways at the time, so they traveled up the Pacific Coast on Highway 1, a two lane road.

The trip was a blend of guy humor, the radio blasting rock and roll music (the songs we now think of as classics), and a euphoric feeling of independence—just two wild and

Oxy looked like this before her ill-fated trip…

crazy guys off to see the world—well, Canada anyway. By day they enjoyed the ocean view, jumped off rocks into the water, and even drove through a big redwood tree. At night they slept in the car. Finally, they arrived at the Puget Sound area in Washington and ferried across the water into Canada. Congratulating each other for reaching their destination they announced, "Mission accomplished."

The trip home was not without a few adventures. Funds were low so they picked berries on the side of the road to eat and painted house numbers on people's curbs or mailboxes to earn money for gas.

Somewhere in the middle of nowhere north of Eureka, California smoke started billowing into the car through the steering column. With no gas or service stations around, they pulled over and dismantled the steering column. Everything looked fine so they put it back together and started driving again.

A short time later the floorboard on the driver's side became quite hot and again smoke started wafting into the car. Searching the car for something to cool off the floorboard, they found some water and two squirt guns (never leave home without your squirt guns), so they filled the squirt guns with water and kept shooting at the floorboard to cool it down. Soon the water didn't seem to do the trick, so they pulled over to the side of the road to survey the situation.

Lifting the hood they discovered the engine manifold had broken. Flames from the engine were shooting directly onto the floorboard, catching the insulation on fire. Finding a tin can on the side of the road, they wired it to cover the hole in the broken manifold. Since the can contained the fire, they didn't need to keep squirting water on the floorboard. Problem solved.

They kept driving.

Next, the overdrive in the transmission started giving them trouble. The car wouldn't stay in gear, forcing Zorro to repeatedly accelerate and coast. Eventually, they came to a gas station in a little poke 'n plum town. You know what a poke 'n plum town is? You poke your head out the window and you are plum out of town.

Knowing it would cost a fortune to fix a transmission and they didn't have much money, they prayed before going into the gas station. After a mechanic examined the car he discovered all it needed was a fuse for the transmission's overdrive. The cost: ten cents. God is good!

All went well until they reached the Grapevine, that long steep incline coming into the mountains surrounding Los Angeles. The car gradually lost power, going slower and slower, even in passing gear. Unaware that they had run very low on oil and were burning out the front main bearings, they limped into Los Angeles at a top speed of thirty miles an hour. Needless to say, the Nash Ambassador was laid to rest in the local junk yard.

They returned home safe and sound, and triumphant at having survived the journey, which in retrospect may have been a minor miracle.

There is a parallel for all of us in this story because our lives are a journey. Our life's journey is like driving down a highway or road. We ride though hills, mountains, and valleys. Sometimes the roads are paved; sometimes they aren't. Sometimes we don't know which way to go. There are unexpected curves and bends. Road work takes us on detours. We might have an accident because we are going too fast. People might honk at us for going too slow. Sometimes we misread signs. Sometimes the signs mislead us.

Looking back on roads we've traveled, we visualize memories accumulated from our experiences. These memories become stories we share. Some stories might reflect good things; some might be bad. Some might be funny; some might be funny now but weren't funny when they happened. When you marry a man like Zorro you have a lot of those kinds of stories in your life.

Most of life's stories are not about what happens when we reach our destination. Usually they're about what happened on the way there or back. Maybe that's because life is not a destination but a trip—a journey. We might not even reach our intended destination, but that doesn't make the stories or the journey less meaningful. Moses never reached the Promised Land, but he had quite a journey, filled with life lessons for all of us today—and God loved him very much (Deut. 34:10-13 KJV).

If we aren't careful, we can live our Christian lives on hold in anticipation of the future coming of Christ. We miss the fact that he is already with us now (Luke 17:21 KJV). He isn't some future destination. He's with us on the trip. And it's a good thing he is. No telling where we would end up if he wasn't.

About twenty years later Zorro and I were assigned to pastor churches in the very Washington area he had traveled to as a teen. Revisiting the Puget Sound ferry he and Mitch had taken into Canada, we noticed two signs at the dock. One read "Ferry to Bremerton" and the other was "Ferry to Canada." Upon closer inspection Zorro made a startling discovery. Evidently they had taken the ferry to Bremerton thinking it was in Canada. Actually, Bremerton is in another part of Washington State. All these years they thought they had been to Canada.

Lucky for them that life is a trip, because they never reached their destination.

Zorro and Mitch twenty years after their "trip to Canada:"
Mitch came to visit us in Washington and they took the
right ferry into Canada this time.

CHAPTER 6

ON THE ROAD AGAIN

*"... you must lead my people across the Jordan River
into the land I am giving them."*

—Joshua 1:2 (NLT)

WE SPENT TEN or so years living in Appalachian areas and I'm not saying the roads were bad but they did leave a lot to be desired. Okay, they were bad.

The "road" stories I could tell are too many to mention. When we first moved to West Virginia we were traveling late at night on a two-lane, curvy, mountainous road. Being impatient, I asked Zorro why he was driving so slowly. He said, "Because I want to be sure the road hasn't washed down the mountain." Sure enough, we happened onto a section where a large chunk of our lane was gone.

In Kentucky we had to drive down a creek bed to visit a person who looked just like a character called Mammy Yokum, from the old Li'l Abner comic strip replete with corn cob pipe and coffee can spittoon. Once while driving on a small road on the side of a snowy mountain to get to a church member's house, our car slid and perched itself half on the road and half dangling a bit off the road, not quite as bad as the movie *Cliffhanger* but enough to be concerned for our lives. Fortunately, the part in mid-air was on Zorro's side so I crawled out my side of the car with our two daughters, age seven months and two years. We trudged down the road to the farm house. The owners and I pondered how to rescue Zorro or if we would ever see him again when all of a sudden we heard a car coming. Miracle of miracles— it was Zorro. Say what you will about the man, but Zorro sure can drive a car.

My favorite road story happened in West Virginia when Zorro was an assistant pastor and I wasn't even in the car. The pastor that Zorro assisted had his own idiosyncrasies. He was a little more bizarre than most, but to each his own. Even if he had passengers with him, he never used his car heater in the winter or his air conditioner in the summer. His favorite snack was raw, hard wheat berries which he liked to munch on all day long as he and Zorro traveled. The *only* advice he ever gave people was to "pray about it." Being young at the time we thought this advice too simplistic but now that we are much older and wiser we find it deep and profound. Yes, Wheat Berry Man was a praying man and gave Zorro a faith lesson he would never forget.

One day, Zorro and Wheat Berry Man were out visiting the flock. Some country roads in West Virginia didn't automatically "take you home to the place you belong." Once in a while they took you where you didn't belong. Such was the case when the guys turned down a dirt road on that sunny autumn day. The road started out fine with two lanes and a little gravel. Gradually what had looked like a small wooded area became a forest. The briar-lined road got narrower and narrower. The trees and briars seemed to engulf them as the road became so downwardly steep and so narrow it was impossible to turn around. They had no choice but to forge ahead. Big ruts appeared in the road. The ruts got bigger and deeper, so much so that the car could go no further.

Wheat Berry Man told Zorro to get the jack out of the trunk. Zorro jacked up the front of the car and Wheat Berry Man drove over the jack to make a little progress. This went on for about an hour or so, until they reach enough level dirt surface to drive on again. They eased down the narrow road until suddenly it opened up and before them appeared a large body of water. The road went right down to the water and stopped. Across the water you could see where the road continued.

Later they found out the name of the waterway was Strange Creek. Yes, that's right. I didn't make that up. Strange Creek flows into the Elk River.

Looking around they saw on their side of the creek a four-wheeler with the highest suspension imaginable parked next to a lone house up a slight hill. A large sign had the word "Ponderosa" embedded into it. Not seeing Little Joe or Hoss around, Zorro walked up to the front door and knocked. A burly man opened the door and said, "You're lost, aren't you?" I guess they didn't get many visitors in their neck of the woods.

Zorro said, "How do we get out of here?"

"There's only one way. You have to cross that creek."

Zorro glanced at their low to the ground '73 Plymouth Fury then back at the man's four-wheel drive with very high suspension. "Can't we just live here with you?"

The man said there was a cement platform under water where the road passed through the creek and continued to the other side where they could see the road emerge out of the water. There was only one teensy weensy problem. If you veered too much to the left or right you and your car would drop off the concrete and sink into the water.

Although it was a creek, it was over a hundred feet wide due to the rainy season and seemed more like a rushing river. They could see it was fairly deep by the steady movement of the flowing water. Wheat Berry Man, being the senior pastor, said, "Let's go for it." He had no fear and great faith. After a little prayer, they got in the car and drove into the water. The level of the water was such that Zorro could put his hand out the window and touch it without lifting out of his seat. How the motor kept running in water that deep is still a mystery. The car did not veer to the right or left but I'm sure a few angels got wet that day keeping those guys on the straight and narrow.

Out the other side they came. Feeling like they just crossed the Jordon to the land of milk and honey, they jubilantly continued their journey. Praise the Lord and pass the wheat berries! Proving once again that God may allow you to go on the road less traveled, but he will always be with you on your journey.

There was a Ponderosa sign, but Little Joe and Hoss didn't live on the banks of Strange Creek.

CHAPTER 7

THE PICNIC

"Go to the ant, thou sluggard; consider her ways,
and be wise:"

—Proverbs 6:6 (KJV)

PEOPLE CANNOT CALL themselves church members unless they have attended a church picnic. Actually, you have to attend quite a few to be considered spiritual or holy. I have attended many picnics through the years, but my holiness is somewhat tainted by the fact that I hate picnics.

This admission could be tantamount to sacrilege. Perhaps *hate* is too strong a word. Let's just say I am not really a picnic-type person. To me it is counterproductive to dirty up your kitchen; place your food, silverware, drinks, plates and tablecloths in baskets and coolers; load it all in a car; haul it to a wooded area; and share it with every bug in the neighborhood, including ants who sing, "The ants go marching two by two, hurrah, hurrah," as they carry your goodies away.

Ants are social creatures that live and work together in harmony as they develop their colonies. They are industrious as they forage your food. Did you know some ants can carry up to fifty times their body weight? It almost seems a shame to kill them, but hey—that's part of the fun of picnics!

I know most people think a picnic is a beautiful family outing and church bonding experience. To me it will always be a potluck with flies and ants. With that said, I have to admit I have learned a few life lessons over the years because of church picnics.

About thirty-five years ago, when we first started working in Valdosta, Georgia, Zorro, a great picnic lover, announced to the congregation his plan for a church picnic. He thought this would be a swell way for us to get to know everyone. He also said it would be a potluck.

We were bombarded with people after church thanking us for our benevolence. Imagine our surprise when we found out the term *potluck* in that particular area (in those days, anyway) meant we would provide all the food. In other words, when everyone shows up they just eat whatever you happen to have in your "pot." By church definition, potluck to us had always meant all people bring food to share.

So I made the following note: Life Lesson No. 1—Be careful about terminology in new areas.

Many years later we worked in London, Kentucky, and the men were to make all the desserts at our yearly picnic. One memorable dessert was a delicious looking chocolate cake. Actually the cake was a cake tin turned upside down and frosted. So each time someone came through the food line and tried to cut it, they hit metal. Another dessert was a yummy looking frosted sponge cake that turned out to be—you guessed it—a frosted sponge. This cake appeared to be a real cake because of its springiness. We got a lot of laughs watching everyone try to cut through that one. Many were quite determined to get a piece of that cake! Some joker made a mud pie with real mud and thought it was hilarious. So I made the following note: Life Lesson No. 2—Men have a warped sense of humor.

My favorite picnic story occurred in Detroit, Michigan, where the annual picnic was a highlight for the children. One of our members worked at a toy factory. Each year the factory donated toys for us to distribute to kids at our picnic. One year I ran a little late getting everything ready— you know, cooking the food; putting it and the silverware, drinks, plates and tablecloths in baskets and coolers; and getting it all in a car so we could haul it to a wooded area to share with the ants. So we decided Zorro would go ahead in our van loaded with the toys and I would soon follow.

He made a quick stop for gas and headed for the park. It wasn't long before he noticed an angry man in a little white car pulling up next to him, pointing to him to pull over. The little white car was actually trying to force Zorro off the road. Zorro was not about to pull over for some crazy guy. So he started praying for God to send a police officer. Lo and behold, within minutes Zorro saw a police car in his rearview mirror. Lights were flashing, sirens were blaring, and Zorro was thanking God for answering his prayer so quickly.

The police pulled up behind Zorro's van and motioned for him to pull over. Zorro thought the police needed to go after the angry guy in the white car but wanting to observe the law; he pulled over to the side of the road. The policeman walked up to Zorro's window, looked him square in the eye and said, "Do you make a habit of not paying for your gas?"

Zorro was dumbfounded, but it all began to make sense. He remembered going into the office of the gas station to pay for his gas with a credit card, but the man said, "Just pay afterwards." In a hurry to get to the picnic, Zorro had filled up, hopped in the van and hit the road.

By now the man in the little white car had pulled over too. He was the owner of the gas station and had called the police. Zorro apologized profusely. The policeman told Zorro the owner would not press charges if he would return to the gas station and pay for his gas. So that's what he did.

At the gas station, Zorro paid up and asked the owner if he had kids. He did, so Zorro opened the back of the van displaying all the toys and told him to take his pick. This made the angry owner very happy. He did share with Zorro that had he not looked like a clean-cut, decent-type guy, he might have legally shot him for robbery. Boy, was Zorro glad he showered and shaved that morning!

I made another note: Life Lesson No. 3—God always answers your prayers—and the other guy's too!

After Zorro's car chase, the kids loved receiving the donated toys at our church picnic in Detroit.

CHAPTER 8

HAVE BUS WILL TRAVEL

"Cast thy burden upon the Lord ..."

—Psalm 55:22 (KJV)

YEARS AGO, A church bus was a mainstay of a congregation—especially if you lived in a rural area like we did in Kentucky. We've had a bus or two in our time, and they served us well.

However, our church buses were never Greyhounds or charter vehicles replete with reclining chairs and restrooms. More often than not they were old, retired, yellow school buses, purchased at a bargain basement price, all in desperate need of face-lifts and overhauls.

"What a deal!" we'd say. And after a new coat of paint—anything but yellow—and an engine rebuild, we were good to go. Our motto was "Have Bus Will Travel."

A good church bus—one that was running—could offer many benefits for a rural congregation. It provided transportation to church for those who did not have another way to get there. When our denomination had week-long festivals in various parts of the country, the church bus allowed many to attend who could not afford to go. If we had get-togethers with churches in other areas or activities several hours away, we would park our cars in a designated area so we all could ride together on the bus, a sort of "park and ride" before the term "park and ride" became vogue. We were so ahead of our time.

A church bus also provided much more than cheap transportation. A true bond was formed among our member-ship. Whether you want to or not, you connect with your neighbor when you're bouncing down the highway. This camaraderie and fellowship built friendships. We'd share coolers of drinks and snacks, play games, and sing songs. The bumpier the ride, the happier the sing-a-long.

Now a church bus needs a good mechanic—actually it needs a great mechanic. Homer was a great mechanic. Short and stocky, Homer was full of faith and enthusiasm. Once he read the scripture about anointing the sick with oil. Homer's cow was very sick and his family needed that cow badly. Many laughed when Homer poured oil on the cow's head and prayed a prayer of faith. They stopped laughing when that cow got well immediately. This was just the kind of faith we needed in a church bus mechanic.

Zorro did a lot of youth work in those days. Each year, Zorro and Homer took teens to our church summer camp in Minnesota. The camp was near the Canadian border and lasted three weeks. They picked up teens from other areas en route, thus supplying affordable rides for many who might not have been able to attend. The ride took about three days from Kentucky.

On one particular trip, the bus broke down next to a large field just outside of Cincinnati, Ohio. A church bus breakdown was no big surprise. Our church bus would do this from time to time. Without fail, the breakdown seemed to happen in the middle of nowhere. That's why you never want to take a trip without your great mechanic on board.

Once we made the mistake of sending an auto parts store owner on one of these trips, thinking this was synonymous with being a mechanic. Not true. When the bus broke down and he looked under the hood, he was clueless as to how to fix it. However, he could point to each car part and tell us how much it would cost if it needed to be replaced, which was not real helpful in the middle of nowhere.

So there they were outside of Cincinnati. Homer hopped out of the bus, opened the hood, and started poking at the engine. Soon he lodged something loose, threw it in the overgrown field, and said, "We don't need that." He went back to fiddling with the engine, another part fell off. Again, Homer threw it in the field and said, "We don't need that either."

Now these weren't little nuts and bolts. They looked like major things you might need to keep a vehicle running. I'm not sure how many parts he tossed away, but enough to have Zorro concerned. Then he connected a few wires and said, "Start her up!"

Zorro tentatively got behind the wheel, turned the key in the ignition, and "vroom, vroom," the engine started right up and purred like a kitten. There were no further mishaps and the church bus buzzed down the road as smooth as could be.

Zorro and I learned a big lesson that day. We've thought many times about how we encumber ourselves with things we feel are so necessary in life. We carry burdens we do not need to bear instead of casting them on God who willingly bears them for us. We weigh ourselves down with extraneous things we feel we need to keep functioning in today's society. Much of what we think is necessary may not be vital at all. You might be surprised to learn how much you can let go of and still buzz down the road of life purring like a kitten. Perhaps you can travel a little faster because the load is lighter.

Somewhere along the journey, church buses became more of a liability than an asset. Litigation-happy people targeted them for giant lawsuits, thinking they could get big bucks suing a church. Now, only very rich churches can afford buses. They usually get something like a Greyhound or luxurious charter vehicle, not a fixer upper, schoolyard reject like we used to have.

I learned a lot about life's journey riding in an old, uncomfortable church bus. "Have Bus Will Travel" was our motto, but it represented more than just getting from one place to another. That motto taught us how to enjoy the ride.

"Have Bus Will Travel" was our motto when we rode in this old church bus.

CHAPTER 9

YOUNG AT HEART

*"Verily I say unto you, Except ye be converted, and
become as little children, ye shall not enter into
the kingdom of heaven."*

—Matthew 18:3 (KJV)

ZORRO HAS A wonderful rapport with kids, so we've
done a lot of youth work at camps and locally through
the years. I think this rapport comes from Zorro never los-
ing those endearing, childlike qualities God smiles on such
as a positive outlook, trusting heart, humility, quickness to
forgive, spontaneity, and really loving to have fun. Which are
all wonderful characteristics, but they can sometimes annoy
your wife. But in all fairness, almost anything a husband
does can annoy his wife.

Zorro and I tend to differ in our approach to life. He
might stop to pick daisies on the side of the road whereas I
would think, "Doesn't he know we're going to be late?" He
might delight in stomping through a puddle in the rain or

making snow angels whereas I would think, "What a mess! Who's going to wash those pants?"

Years ago we were bringing teens back from a weekend ski outing on a Sunday night when Zorro started a snowball fight at a rest area. The kids loved it, but soon retreated to the cars. I can still hear them begging him, "Please, take us home. We have homework to finish."

Once during a balloon fight at a church picnic, our daughter Sherisa was asked, "What would your father say if he could see you?" Someone is always trying to lay a guilt trip on a PK (pastor's kid). Sherisa said, "He'd probably say, 'Quick! Fill one up for me. I think I've got a good shot at this guy.'"

And when our daughter Shelly was little, I tried to get her to go to sleep by threatening, "Do you want me to go get your father?"

She said, "I wish you would. I think he'd let me stay up a little longer."

Teen trips for our local congregations have always been part of our ministry. We've taken teens from West Virginia and Kentucky to Florida where they've seen Disney World, Cypress Gardens, and floated down Ichetucknee Springs in inner tubes. We've taken teens from Washington and California to Hawaii where they've stayed on the beach, visited the Polynesian Cultural Center, and toured pineapple plantations. We've taken teens from Michigan to Washington, D.C. where they've seen the Smithsonian, visited Arlington Cemetery, and toured the White House.

I have such fond memories of the White House. Our son Matthew was about nine at the time. He got ill on the tour. The secret service men took him outside for some air, where he promptly barfed behind a big bush. I always get a twinge when I see photos of the shrubs around the White House. Matthew christened the one on the left.

Zorro and Matthew take it easy after Matthew barfed on the
White House tour in Washington, D.C.

We've received some lovely notes from teens we've
worked with appreciating Zorro's heart for children. They
are grown now with kids and grandkids of their own. Phyllis
Warren from Kentucky wrote, "I was one of those that probably wouldn't have gone anywhere if Mr. D hadn't had a
compassion for kids. One of my favorite memories is when
he took a bunch of us to West Virginia. We played games
all day, ate all we wanted, and got to meet other teens from
other churches. The girls slept on the floor in an upstairs
room of someone's house; (I can't remember where the
guys stayed) and rode home with a carload of other teens
(after the all day picnic and fun) in a car that was colder
than a well-diggers rear because the heat didn't work. Ah,
memories! Those were some great times."

Trying to make these trips affordable was a challenge, so we didn't always eat the best cuisine or stay in posh accommodations. You might even call us cheap. One such "cheap" trip occurred when we took our Detroit teens to Florida. We found a conveniently located, old camp-like facility with two dormitory-like buildings (one for the boys and one for the girls) and several rooms with bunk beds (we'd bring our own sheets) plus a separate kitchen. Each dorm had one bathroom and one shower at the end of a hallway. The buildings were old, but functional and we would use the camp as our base of operation. We'd eat breakfast there, leave for the day to see sights, go to the beach or have activities, and return to fix our own dinners to save money. The best part was this place was so affordable.

Well, this place was so bad they should have paid us to stay there. Not because it was dirty, but because it was very, very old. The minimal décor was not even up to Good Will standards. Posted on one wall by the bathroom was a list of rules. Our favorite was: Under no circumstances should you take any items from the camp home with you, including curtains or pictures. As a couple of chaperones and I waited to get in the bathroom one looked at the rules and pointed to a 2,000-year-old, plastic curtain covering the window and said, "I'm so disappointed because I really wanted to take this home."

To make matters worse, Florida was having a heat wave. It was hotter than (excuse my vernacular, but there is just no other way to describe it) hell and of course, there was no air conditioning. The rooms had very little ventilation. Sleeping was difficult. Not only was it stifling, but the sweat literally poured off us as we tried to find some comfort. If you could open a window, there was no breeze, only mosquitoes—the really big ones that say, "Should we eat him here or take him with us?" My souvenir for the trip was an electric fan I bought at K-Mart.

In spite of all the hardships and complaining, the teens seemed to have a great time. Ah, the resiliency of youth! However, the chaperones were the ones who really suffered. This was evident at the beach when the teens said, "Let's throw Mrs. D in the water!"

Sometimes teens mistakenly think Zorro and I have the same easy-going disposition. I yelled, "If you do, I'll see to it that you never get another teen trip like this again."

The kids backed off immediately, but all the other chaperones chanted, "Throw her in! Throw her in!"

We survived and managed to take these same teens on other trips, but none remotely as bad as this one. Years later we took a teen survey to gather info for making future plans. Several stated this Florida trip was the best trip ever. One went so far as to say we needed more trips like this one.

I'm glad they had fond memories but wondered if I had been on the same trip? Were they just idealizing the past or having a distorted view? Sometimes the worse the trip is, the more vivid the memory. Maybe they were just glad someone cared enough to take them on a trip.

Children look on the bright side, can be content no matter what, and can have a good time in spite of the circumstances. No wonder God says to become as little children. I can't help but think the world would be a better place if we were all a little more young at heart.

CHAPTER 10

ALOHA

"Delight thyself also in the Lord; and he shall give thee the desires of thine heart."

—Psalm 37:4 (KJV)

WHEN WE WORKED on the west coast in the Tacoma and Olympia, Washington area, Zorro thought a youth trip to Hawaii would be educational and fun. Most had never been to Hawaii so they were delighted. Many adults in those congregations had not been to Hawaii either so we had quite a few volunteers to chaperone, eighty-four of us in total.

Usually our trips are a myriad of uncomfortable accommodations, cramped travel, and tons of fast food. This trip was an exception. The pastor in Hawaii had found a former army barracks that had been converted into a camp for traveling groups. It wasn't the Hilton, but located on the beach near the Polynesian Cultural Center. When we weren't touring we could swim and play beach volleyball.

They even provided the equipment. Not only was the price right, but it included three meals a day that we didn't have to prepare. This was *not* going to be our average youth trip. Praise God!

The kids worked hard for about a year having bake sales, selling candy and citrus fruit to earn money to go. We decided to use a booking agent from Hawaii to make our travel arrangements and had just sent him our money. A month before we were scheduled to leave, everyone was euphoric. Then we received the phone call. The booking agent's company had gone into receivership. Our travel money was in this company's account and now frozen. We thought we would have to cancel the trip. Being the pessimistic spouse that I am I said, "I knew it was too good to be true!"

However, Zorro decided not to give up hope and sprang into action. He contacted our church "hotline" and told everyone to pray and fast about the situation. God is infinite and powerful. In the scheme of worldwide problems our little trip to Hawaii was not earth shattering, but on the other hand God does care about the intimate details of our lives. Maybe we just needed to let him know we would place the situation in his loving hands, trust him, and accept his decision.

About a week later Zorro received another call from our booking agent who, incidentally, just worked for the company and was not the owner. He was heart sick about what had happened to us. The receivership had not been lifted but he couldn't stop thinking about all those kids who worked for a year to save money for this trip. He told Zorro he was taking a second mortgage on his house and sending our money back so we could make our own air flight arrangements. Zorro told him he didn't have to do that, but the man insisted. He just felt it was something he needed to do. Much rejoicing resounded throughout Tacoma and

Olympia that night. Our church "hotline" was buzzing with glory hallelujahs.

We scrambled to find good deals at different airlines on such short notice. One bargain included a free rental car with ticket purchase. We ended up with twice as many rental car vouchers than drivers. We were able to trade them in and upgrade our compact cars to vans, Cadillacs and other luxury automobiles. Not only did we drive around Hawaii in style in our expensive vehicles, but we swam in the ocean, soaked up some sun, played volleyball, explored a pineapple plantation, visited the Polynesian Cultural Center, and one night even had a dance under the stars on the beach because someone brought his boom box.

When God blesses you, it really does overflow. The thought that God had heard our prayers made this trip very special, indeed. It's as if he said, "Aloha! Have a wonderful time on me!" And we did!

Shelly, me, Zorro, and Sherisa go native in Hawaii.

CHAPTER 11

THE VIP COMETH

*"...for he maketh his sun to rise...and sendeth rain
on the just and on the unjust."*

—Matthew 5:45 (KJV)

W E HAD JUST moved to Michigan when we were in-
formed that Zorro would be the local coordinator of
a visit from our denominational leader at the time whom
we will just call Mr. VIP. Surrounding churches were invited
to Detroit for a combined church service and in a gesture of
appreciation to the ministry, Mr. VIP would host an elegant
dinner that evening. Mr. VIP had made a number of these
trips. So to help answer procedure questions, those making arrangements from headquarters compiled a book of
instructions to aid the local coordinator. We thought this
was a great idea—until we received it.

Now when I say book, I do not mean pamphlet. This
quite thick book contained everything you needed to know
about a VIP's visit to your area, from the air pressure in the

tires of the specific rental vehicle designated to pick him up at the airport, to the fresh squeezed mango juice waiting in his room when he arrived—nothing was left to chance.

As a side note, having known Mr.VIP personally he would have probably been happier with a diet Coke than exotic juice, but those surrounding him wanted him well cared for. I don't think we ever found fresh squeezed mango juice in Detroit at the time. Maybe we substituted carrot juice and hoped they wouldn't notice the difference.

As extreme as this book may have seemed, having a plan to follow made things easier. The "book" came in mighty handy when other ministers asked us why we didn't do something differently. We just smiled and said, "It's not in the book."

In those days, Mr. VIP was taking a lot of trips so he traveled in a small, private jet. According to the "book," Zorro, as the coordinator, was assigned to greet him at the airport. Our six-year-old son Matthew and I accompanied him. My instructions to Matthew were specific. Do not speak unless you are spoken to. Keep your mouth shut. Zip up your lips. I asked him if he understood what I meant. In accordance with my instructions he did not speak to answer me, but nodded in complete agreement.

At the airport we exchanged pleasantries with Mr. VIP and he invited us aboard the jet for a private tour. A grin spread across Matthew's face and his eyes sparkled. I could tell he was excited. The plane was not that large or impressive but to a six-year-old it must have seemed enormous. Mr. VIP was showing us the cockpit when he made the fatal mistake of asking Matthew some obscure question. Perceiving this as some sort of permission to speak, Matthew proceeded to talk his little head off in spite of my best "I'm gonna kill you when I get you home" look. What a joy children are.

Zorro and me with our backs to the camera on the right
hand side as we greet the VIPs.

We got Mr. VIP and his entourage all settled for the
night, then we proceeded with the final preparations for
the church service and dinner the next day. With just about
all of our churches in Michigan coming, there was much to
do. A combined pre-teen choir from all the churches was
scheduled to sing one of Mr. VIP's favorite songs, *Glorious
Things of Thee Are Spoken,* so rehearsal was needed. We
needed a final meeting with the Renaissance Center where
the service would be held. We had endless details to attend
to and in all honesty, if three other full-time ministers in
the Detroit area hadn't helped us, we would still be trying
to sort everything out. Finally, it dawned on the day of the
event.

At least I think it dawned. I wasn't sure because of the
rain.

As coordinator, Zorro's job was to ride with Mr. VIP to
the Renaissance Center. Accompanying Mr. VIP was his dear
friend whom we will just call Joe. Mr. VIP was sharing with

Joe some of the stories he had heard about Zorro. Mr. VIP spoke to Zorro and smiled: "Now aren't you the one who left his wife at the gas station for six hours?"

Zorro, a little embarrassed, replied: "Well, yes that was me."

Joe: "I don't believe it!"

Mr. VIP laughed and said: "And didn't your car get stolen one time when you were dressed up like Zorro?"

Zorro, lowering his head: "Well, yes that was me."

Joe: "I don't believe it!"

Mr. VIP laughed louder and said: "And didn't you blow a balloon up at church and it flew out over the audience and it came back and landed on your head?"

Zorro, looking sheepish: "Well, yes that was me, too."

Joe: "I just don't believe it!"

Obviously, some of these Zorro stories had spread further than we hoped, so Zorro felt relieved when the conversation was cut short by their arrival at the Renaissance Center. Zorro, being well prepared, hopped out of the car with a huge umbrella to shield Mr. VIP from the pouring rain. Just as Mr. VIP got out of the car under the umbrella, a big gust of wind came and suddenly blew the umbrella inside out. Our VIP and his dear friend stood in the pouring rain. What were the odds? Mr. VIP just grinned. Our instruction book didn't cover what to do when you've just drenched your denominational leader. Joe turned to Zorro and said, "I believe all that stuff really did happen to you!"

Proving once again that it rains on the lowly and the VIPs in the world—and God does have a sense of humor.

CHAPTER 12

NIGERIA OR BUST

"And he said, 'Let us take our journey, and let us go,
and I will go before thee.'"

—Genesis 33:12 (KJV)

IN YEARS PAST, our church has provided many occasions
for travel. We used to have a worldwide fall festival and
one year our family volunteered to go to a foreign country
if they needed someone to help. Since we had not traveled
much we thought it would be an educational opportunity
for our children plus a chance to serve others out of our
comfort zone. At first we were told we were too late, but
then we received a call saying they did have an opening for
Nigeria in Africa. We were asked if we were interested.

After a family discussion, we enthusiastically said, "Yes!"
Our daughters, Shelly and Sherisa, were in college at the
time so we would have to pay their way, but the church
would cover expenses for Zorro, our twelve-year-old son
Matthew, and me. We scraped the money together for the

girls and made plans for the trip. Since we had not traveled abroad before, we were excited about the prospect of adventure.

In retrospect, there were certain clues that perhaps this would not be an ideal family trip, but there's a kind of naïveté that comes with inexperience and blind trust—a fine line separating faith and foolishness. Which is just another way of saying, "Boy, were we stupid or what?"

Clue No. 1—When one receives a last-minute call to go somewhere, one should always ask why there is an opening.

Clue No. 2—Nigeria's political and socio-economic situation in 1993 was tenuous at best. In fact the Lagos, Nigeria airport was considered so dangerous the United States had suspended all flights there. Perhaps that's why we were flying British Air?

No one at our headquarters seemed concerned about this. I did receive a call from a friend, the wife friend of a VIP, who said, "Barbara, you don't have to go on this trip, you know." But we were so enthralled with the thought of travel, I just replied, "They wouldn't send us anywhere dangerous, would they?"

Clue No. 3—We would need vaccinations, passports, and visas. However, when applying for the visas we were instructed not to say anything about being a minister or going to a religious convention. We would receive a letter from a "personal friend" in Nigeria inviting us for a visit. We were going to Nigeria for a "vacation."

Clue No. 4—Yes, we could bring gifts for the children such as pencils, crayons, books, toys, candy, clothing, etc. However, if these things were found in our suitcases during the customs check entering Nigeria, they would be confiscated.

We were a bit concerned because our visas hadn't arrived. One day before our scheduled departure panic set in.
Still no visas so we asked everyone to pray. Our visas arrived
the very morning we were due to fly out of California. Talk
about cutting it close. They had plenty of time to issue our
visas, but we found out this was the Nigerian Embassy's little
way of letting you know they are in control. Also, Nigeria,
like many foreign countries, is not as time-conscious as the
United States.

Our congregation was so thrilled about sending items
to the youth in Africa that we ended up taking ten suitcases
and five carry-ons. Looking a little like a movie advertise-
ment for "Ma and Pa Kettle and Family Visit Africa," we
headed for the airport.

Clue No. 5—At the airport in San Francisco, a huge
disclaimer about not being responsible for anyone traveling to Lagos, Nigeria hung in the lobby. "Well, it's a little
late now," I thought. I was beginning to have visions of the
powers that be from headquarters waving good-bye to us
and saying, "Bon Voyage and hope you don't die!"

Off we went to our British offices in London where we
would be given further instructions. In London, we voiced a
little concern about this trip since we were so inexperienced.
"Not to worry," they said. "We've arranged for you to meet
someone on the plane who is an old hand at all this."

Clue No. 6—Our contact on the plane would take care
of us until we arrived in Nigeria. Once in Nigeria we would
recognize our other contact by a certain magazine he or
she would be carrying. This was beginning to sound like a
James Bond movie.

Clue No. 7—"And by the way, would you please get this
money into Nigeria without it being confiscated?" Maybe
this was a James Bond movie. The family gave this a little
thought and decided to divide the money three ways and

stuff it in Shelly, Sherisa, and my bras. We had never felt so well-endowed.

Clue No. 8—When we went through the passport check at Gatwick Airport, the British official asked why we were going to Nigeria. We said, "For a vacation!" He laughed and replied in a British accent, "No one goes to Nigeria for holiday."

Clue No. 9—When we met our "someone on the plane who is an old hand at this," he was not as experienced as we hoped. He said, "This is my first time. They told me you knew what you were doing and would guide me through everything."

Clue No. 10—Getting off the plane that night in Nigeria was like entering a military state. Uniformed officers with machine guns stood everywhere. After a two-hour wait in 95-degree heat, we finally reached the passport and visa check area. A language barrier caused some problems next. The man did not want to let us through unless we paid money. He said, "I am an official!" Zorro looked confused and gave him a dollar. The man scoffed and said, "I am a HIGH official!" Zorro sheepish replied, "Do you take Master Card?" Miraculously, the man laughed and let us through. We found out later that these bribes were commonplace in this part of the country.

Clue No. 11—It took another hour to get our luggage. We headed for customs fearing all our gifts to the children would be taken and praying they wouldn't strip search us and find the money. The customs official looked at all our luggage. He chose to inspect one of Shelly's smaller bags, one filled with just her clothes. Another miracle! He let us pass through.

We trudged out the door—hot, tired, thirsty, and laden down like pack mules. Like a vision, we spotted a woman prominently carrying the magazine we were told to look for in her hand. Praise God. The clueless Dahlgrens had arrived.

Saying, "Yes, we'll go to Nigeria" may not have been the most sensible decision we ever made. But we remembered what God told the Israelites in Deuteronomy 31:6. "Be strong and courageous! Do not be afraid of them! The Lord your God will go ahead of you. He will neither fail you nor forsake you (NLT)." We might be clueless at times, but God isn't. It was comforting to know that wherever our Christian journey was taking us, God would be right by our sides.

San Jose Mercury News • **World/People** • Saturday, November 20, 199

Diplomats call Nigerian crisis worst in decades

BY JOHN DARNTON
New York Times

LONDON — With the generals once again in open and absolute command, Nigeria is facing the prospect of economic chaos, political upheaval and perhaps even conflict between its two major tribes, the politically dominant Hausas in the north and the restive Yorubas in the southwest, Nigerians, diplomats and foreign experts say.

strongman, Gen. Sani Abacha. Wednesday, Abacha was installed as Nigeria's seventh military leader since independence from Britain in 1960. He promptly began dismantling the democratic institutions that had been carefully constructed, abolishing national and state assemblies, dissolving the two military-created political parties, removing elected state governors and proscribing all political meetings and associations.

This was the headline shortly after we returned from Nigeria. If it had run before our trip, we might have thought twice about going!

CHAPTER 13

ALMOST BUSTED IN NIGERIA

"Here I am, a stranger in a foreign land..."
—Genesis 23:4 (NLT)

TO SAY WE were clueless about this type of international travel is an understatement. Yet, here we were in Nigeria.

We were greeted by our host family and local ministers Mr. and Mrs. Okai. What a blessing they were for us! They helped us forge our way through a barrage of people wanting money to help us with our luggage. If Mr. and Mrs. Okai had not been with us I'm not sure what would have happened to our suitcases and all the gifts we brought for the children.

Ignoring the beggars proved a difficult task. Some had been maimed by their parents just so they could get more money begging. We had been warned that if we gave money to one, scores would follow us. We learned to say "no" and move on.

The perfect Nigerian hosts: Mr. and Mrs. Okai

On the ride to our hotel, we were given a crash course in surviving our stay. "Crash course" could be taken literally. In Lagos, driving was a unique experience. Lagos did not have many traffic lights, road signs, or stop signs. Drivers made lanes wherever there was an opening, blocked oncoming traffic, and honked at people who got in their way. And people were everywhere—walking in the middle of the street, congregating here and there, spilling out of busses, and hopping off trucks.

Mr. Okai said, "You must be alive to live in Lagos."

At first we thought he meant Lagos was alive with activity, hustle and bustle. Actually, he was cautioning us to stay alert if we wanted to survive in Lagos.

We learned a few guidelines for survival: Stay together. Don't share a taxi with anyone. Don't relinquish your passports to anyone. Don't take pictures around any officials or your camera would be confiscated. Be careful of scams. You might need to bribe people to get things. Learn to dicker at the markets. Time is more of a concept than a reality because nothing ever starts on time. Policemen are not your friends.

Yes, the police were corrupt. A bank robbery took place a couple of weeks before we arrived. As the police chased the thieves, they threw a handful of money in the air. The robbers escaped while the police were busy picking it up and putting it in their pockets.

We were thankful that much of our time would be spent with the Okais because we needed their guidance. However, we stayed at a hotel. Mr. Okai helped us check in and made sure our accommodations were adequate. Shelly, Sherisa, and I sought a bit of privacy so we could dig the contraband money out of our bras. We were glad to finally hand it over to Mr. Okai. We said our good-byes and planned to meet the next day.

Early the next morning we experienced our first scam. Zorro received a phone call from a Dr. Stevens instructing him to leave the hotel and go to the airport immediately because a strike was planned. This ruse was used to get patrons out of the hotel so they could be mugged. This scam was so common that a disclaimer hung in the hotel lobby.

The Okais were most gracious and we found our Nigerian brethren to be well-educated, sincere, dedicated, and a delight. Most spoke several languages. These happy people, victims of a country's poor leadership, truly made this trip worthwhile. Our first time at church they formed a long line and everyone kept saying, "You are welcome"— their way of saying, "We welcome you." They were full of love and generosity, which couldn't have been easy since the average income was approximately a hundred dollars a month.

Conceptual time meant church would usually start "around" ten o'clock or later. The music was lovely. Hearing songs praising God in their native tongue was so inspiring.

Zorro gave great, basic sermons the Nigerians seemed to identify with. Our college-aged daughters were asked to distribute the presents we brought from the United States to the children. Matthew, whom they nicknamed "Mac," bonded well with the other twelve-year-old boys and was content trying to catch the large, red-headed lizards.

Our daughters distributing gifts...

Our trip was a whirlwind of activities, church, meetings, and tours. We ate jollaf rice, noticed people carrying everything from coolers to stacks of wood on their heads, saw humungous anthills, and shopped at open markets. The Nigerian rate of exchange fluctuated a great deal, but while we were there thirty-five naira was the same as one American dollar. Sherisa never quite got the knack for haggling over prices. Even the natives felt sorry for her and were trying to help. One said, "No, no! You don't understand.

You give a price; then I give a price. You give a price; then I give a price."

All in all, the trip had been pleasant and pretty uneventful—until the last day. We were scheduled to go to church in Benin City about two and a half hours away. Later that night we would attend a leadership dinner meeting in Lagos. The road to Benin City was rough and considered dangerous, especially at night when the robbers came out. So we planned to be back in Lagos before dark. We took two cars. One was a hired car from our hotel with a driver named Alfred. The other belonged to the Okais. Our children, along with Sam from church, rode in the hired car. Sam was about the same age as our daughters and would help with communication if anything came up. Zorro and I rode with the Okais.

All went well until the trip home. Alfred's car ran out of gas. Both vehicles had plenty of gas when we started the trip, but Alfred decided to do a little joy riding while the rest of us were at church that day. Here we were in the middle of nowhere, on a dangerous road at dusk. With no gas stations around, we began to pray. Mr. Okai noticed a house in the distance and decided to walk over and see if they had any gas. He negotiated a deal to get us enough gas to make it to Lagos. It cost ten times the going rate, but we were thankful for it.

Our original plan was to drop our children at the hotel where they would eat and pack since we were leaving in the morning. Zorro and I would go to the meeting with the Okais. We had to split up because of the late hour. Sam would come with the Okais and us, and Alfred would take our children to the hotel, which was fairly close. With such a short distance; surely everything would be okay. Alfred had already blown it once that day, so he said he would take Shelly, Sherisa, and Matthew straight to the hotel.

Well, in Alfred's zeal to get Shelly, Sherisa, and Matthew straight to the hotel, he went the wrong way on a one-way street. Granted, the road was not marked clearly since there was no traffic light or sign. This could be viewed as an honest mistake. The five policemen who seemed to come out of nowhere surrounding the car did not see it that way. Some carried machine guns so Alfred had no choice but to stop in the middle of the street. They motioned for Alfred to pull over to the side. He refused so one officer jumped in the unlocked passenger side of the front seat of the car while our children huddled in the back. He yelled at Alfred until he pulled over. They asked for Alfred's license and papers. He would not turn them over. He just kept saying, "Anyone can make a mistake."

This upset the police who started to slap him around. They forced him out of the car. They told him to open the trunk. Alfred refused. They beat him up some more. Our kids were terrified. Matthew had been eating a fruit roll-up which he squeezed so hard purple juice ran down his arm. He asked the girls. "Aren't you scared?" They were scared to death, but just kept reassuring their little brother that God would take care of them.

One officer started letting the air out of the tires, but another told him to stop. One came back to the car and shined a flashlight on the three frightened passengers. "Your driver has broken the law and must pay the penalty. He must go to jail."

The kids agreed. Alfred had proven to be a pain. They asked if Alfred could please take them back to the hotel first. Because of a communication barrier the policeman didn't understand what the girls were saying. "No!" he said.

A different officer poked his head into the window and said, "Your driver is stupid! He is brainless! He will have to pay a fine or go to jail!"

Suddenly a light bulb went off in Shelly's head. "A fine? How much?"

He shouted, "One hundred dollars!"

"We don't have that much."

"How much do you have?"

The girls rummaged through their purses and found 230 naira which was worth about seven dollars. "If I give this to you, will you let Alfred take us back to the hotel?"

He conferred with the other officers. "Okay!" He took the money and handed Sherisa Alfred's papers and license and started to leave.

Alfred got back in the car. "Whew!" They thought. "That was close."

But when Alfred got back in the car, it wouldn't start. Shelly and Sherisa got out and started pushing it. Suddenly the police ran back to them. The girls glanced at each other as if to say, "Oh, no! What now?" They told the girls to get in the car and the policemen pushed the car. They stopped traffic and pushed the car around the entire intersection before it started. As they drove off, the police were actually smiling and waving good-bye.

As soon as our children got into the hotel room, they dropped everything, knelt down, and thanked God for delivering them. That's where we found all three of them when we returned that night—on their knees. They shared their story with us. We all said prayers of thanksgiving.

Our "uneventful" trip was coming to an end. The next day we were scheduled to fly out of Nigeria. What more could possibly happen?

Zorro takes a picture of Sherisa, Shelly, Mr. & Mrs. Okai,
Matthew and me having dinner at the Okai's house.

CHAPTER 14

BUSTING OUT OF NIGERIA

"… when the family of Jacob left that foreign land,"

Psalm 114:1 (NLT)

OUR FLIGHT WAS to leave at eleven in the morning. Mr. Okai and Dennis, the church member who would take us to the airport, met us in the hotel lobby at nine. They assured us we had plenty of time. After all, we were flying on Nigerian Airlines. They rarely leave on time. I wanted to get some postcards, but Mr. Okai said, "Just get them at the airport. You'll have lots of time and they're cheaper. They say you're leaving at eleven but you probably won't leave until three this afternoon."

There was some discrepancy about our bill. It took a little time, but Mr. Okai worked it out with the hotel. I don't know what we would have done without the Okais on this trip. They were truly a blessing from God. We thanked Mr. Okai for a wonderful time and waved good-bye. By the time we got to the airport it was half past ten. Dennis found two men to help with our luggage. He instructed us that no matter what happened we should stay right with our luggage, keep an eye on those men, and do not let our passports out of our sight.

When we got to the check-in counter, it was closed. Dennis found someone to talk to and guess what? The plane really was leaving around eleven. They said we were too late. They handed us some forms to fill out. We rushed with Dennis to the other end of the airport to talk to an official. We showed him our passports. He couldn't help us. We rushed to another official at the other end of the airport. We showed him our passports. We did this about four times. Confusion set in as we tried to hang onto our luggage, which our "helpers" kept deserting, and stay together as a family while rushing back and forth across the airport trying to figure out what was going on.

Soon we had a crowd of officials around us. They were all talking, yelling, and waving their arms in the air. Dennis was pleading for us. Finally, they agreed to let us get on the plane, but not our luggage. However, they might send it on the next flight. Dennis pleaded to get our luggage on this flight but they wouldn't allow it. One official grabbed our passports and told us to follow him. We tried to confer with Dennis. The official was perturbed. "Don't you know I'm trying to help you?"

We weren't so sure. We didn't know who we could trust.

Dennis said to go with the official and get on the plane. He would pray for us and take care of the luggage. We were moved by his godly confidence and bravery. Zorro gave Dennis the airport tax money we were supposed to pay for each piece of luggage and a little extra in case he needed help persuading someone to get our luggage on the plane. We hugged and parted. He would be in our prayers as well.

The last we saw of him, he was struggling with ten suitcases and talking to more officials.

We ran with the official carrying our passports through visa checks, through passport checks, and through radar detectors. All kinds of buzzers went off, but we just followed the man with our passports. One official looked at our passports and said we didn't need this guy leading us. Our leader said, "Yes, they do! I'm a transit officer."

The official gave a look like, "Yeah, right!" But he let us through. We didn't know who to believe.

We were exhausted when we finally reached the boarding area. We saw the short ramp where we should enter the plane. The transit officer said we needed to pay him the airport tax money. Zorro said we gave our money to Dennis to pay the tax. He's the one who had our luggage. The transit officer was upset. "This is a bad man. He has taken your money and run away!"

This upset me, so I said, "You are wrong. He is a good man!"

"You must pay your airport tax to me," the transit officer said. "I will go and find this man!" And off he quickly disappeared through a crowd—with our passports.

Zorro was torn. Should he stay with us or abandon his family to follow the man with our passports? He opted to stay with us.

Now here we were, in a foreign country, all alone, no passports, and in quite a mess. Our family looked at each other, formed a circle, bowed our heads, and prayed. We didn't care who saw us or what they thought.

No sooner had we said "Amen" when our transit officer returned with another official. There was more yelling and hand waving. Suddenly, the co-pilot came to the door. He started shouting at our transit officer. "Let these people pass. Their luggage is loaded. We are behind schedule. It's already eleven fifteen."

We were too stunned to even laugh, having lived with time as more of a concept than a reality for the past week.

Then the pilot appeared and insisted we get on that plane. The transit officer shook his head, "No! They must give me money."

The pilot rushed to the officer, grabbed our passports from his hands, and shoved them at us. "Follow me," he barked.

We grabbed those passports and quickly followed him onto the plane. There we sat—numb from what had happened and having trouble relaxing. We still faced the possibility someone would jerk us off the plane. After a couple of minutes I looked at Zorro and said, "I guess I'll just forget about the post cards."

He smiled.

Then I said, "Do you think our luggage really did make it on board?"

He glanced at the torn, frayed seats and threadbare carpet, then replied, "I wouldn't worry about it. We'll be lucky if the plane makes it."

The small jet looked like a reject from World War II. We clutched our passports. Soon we were in mid-air.

I don't know how Dennis did it, but our luggage arrived safely. And so did we—older, wiser, and with more faith. Some may think we survived by chance, but we know better. We experienced God's deliverance every step of the way.

Perhaps we were foolish to volunteer for this trip. I don't know. I do know our family treasures our time in Nigeria. Our Nigerian brethren inspired us. The kind of deliverance God granted us, they must rely on every day.

Shelly, Sherisa, me, Matthew, and Zorro model our African outfits. We treasured our time in Africa, even though we had some narrow escapes. God is good!

CHAPTER 15

MISSING THE BOAT

"So He said, 'Come.' And when Peter had come down out of the boat, he walked on the water to go to Jesus."

—Matthew 14:29 (NKJ)

WHEN ZORRO AND I started dating, it was apparent water skiing was very important to him. This sport brought him much joy and indeed he was quite adept at trick skiing. In fact, forty years ago there were only a few worldwide who could ski on their bare feet and Zorro was one of them. Zorro probably could have moved to Florida and worked at Cypress Gardens as a water skier when he graduated from college, but his dream was to become a minister. God granted that wish, so we married and our first assignment was, believe it or not, in Jacksonville, Florida, which was close enough to see those Cypress Garden skiers occasionally.

Since water sports have always been in Zorro's veins, naturally he wanted to own a boat. Being in ministry and not being rich and increased with goods, the boats we've had through the years have been—how can I say this delicately—clunkers. Since beauty is in the eye of the beholder and love is blind, Zorro might call them "classics." Clunker or classic? What would you call a boat that starts up fine on land, but doesn't run in water?

A sign of things to come happened while Zorro was in college in Texas. Being fairly fluent in Spanish, he was asked by one of the faculty to guide a campus tour for a group visiting from Mexico. Part of the tour included a large pontoon boat ride on Lake Loma. All went well until he pointed out a big fish in the water on the left side of the boat. As everyone rushed to the left side to see it, the boat tipped in the air. Panic stricken, Zorro yelled, "Get back! Get back!"

But not before one elderly woman toppled into the lake shouting, "Ayudame Dios! Ayudame Dios!" which means, "Help me God! Help me God!" Fortunately she bobbed in the water until Zorro could pull her out.

Years later he was asked to teach water skiing at our denominational summer youth camp in Minnesota. He did this each summer for many, many years. One of the camp highlights was the water ski show they performed for the local community every Fourth of July. One summer while practicing for the show, he propelled off the ski jump and landed in the water the wrong way. At first he felt fine but the caretaker of the camp noticed him holding his head a little sideways and said, "You need to get to the emergency room."

After being examined they found a hairline fracture in his neck vertebra. If it had been one inch to the left or to the right they would have had to put pins in his skull. Fortunately, he only had to wear a cervical collar for the rest of the summer. He was still a little woozy when he looked up at the doctor and said, "Doc, can I ski in the water ski show this Sunday?"

The doctor didn't miss a beat and said, "Why sure! But if you fall remember to hold your head perfectly straight and still, because if you don't—you're gonna die."

Another time in Detroit, Zorro and the pastors we worked near decided to take a fishing trip. Launching Zorro's boat into the St. Clair River on the Canadian/Michigan border, they found a perfect spot for catching "the big ones." As they began to settle in for a day of fishing and male bonding, an ocean liner came by, sucked all the water out from under their boat, and left it tipped on its side in about a foot of water. The guys got out of the boat and tried to push it level and into deeper water so it would float, but the water just seemed to keep rushing away from them. Eventually the water came back and the boat started floating again. They came home with no fish, but stories about "You should have seen the ocean liner that got away."

Of course, the story our grown children love to tell is the time our oldest daughter Shelly was moving into her first apartment. Not able to find a truck to haul her furniture, Zorro decided the boat would make a dandy U-Haul. Shelly must have been anxious to move out and the other two kids might have been casting lots for her room—so there we all were: Zorro, me, and our three kids, Shelly, Sherisa, and Matthew, loading the boat with Shelly's possessions, driving it across town, and praying no one we knew saw us. No wonder Sherisa became a therapist.

Not long ago Zorro conceded boat defeat and got rid of his latest junker. As with so many things in life, letting go is never easy. It saddened him, but most of the time he doesn't miss it.

So imbedded in our family history are these water and boat stories that last year before our family all came home for Christmas, Matthew jokingly lamented the following in an e-mail message: "Too bad we sold the boat. We could have sung Christmas carols while being pulled through town on the boat while dressed up as Bible characters…but I guess that's not an option anymore."

I'm not going to lie to you. I don't miss the boat. I'm glad it's gone. I'm glad they're all gone. Those eye sores were more trouble than they were worth. However, occasionally I see a faraway look in Zorro's eyes, especially when we drive past an SUV pulling a Regal 2000 Bowrider headed for adventure. He quotes scriptures about Jesus calling the fishermen and Peter getting out of the boat to walk on the water. Then I bring him back down to earth by explaining that if Peter had one of Zorro's boats, it would have sunk to the bottom of the Sea of Galilee. The greater miracle would not have been Peter walking on water; it would have been keeping the boat afloat.

Zorro poses on one of his "classic" boats.

CHAPTER 16

A WORD "UNFITLY" SPOKEN

"A word fitly spoken is like apples of gold in pictures of silver."

—Proverbs 25:11 (KJV)

Warning: *This chapter is not for those easily offended at the slightly off-color word. Read at your own risk.*

A MINISTER CAN'T speak before congregations week after week after week for years and not have that little innocent slip of the tongue that happens to all of us. If a minister's faux pax is mildly off-color, it can be a little shocking, thus enhancing the delight people seem to receive from it.

A minister friend of ours was conducting a Bible study with a fellow minister and meant to say, "And Abraham pitched his tent." However it came out, "And Abraham pinched his tit." Everyone gasped and tee-heed. He realized he must have said something wrong so he tried to correct his mistake. Unfortunately he repeated it. The tee-hees turned into giggles. He repeated it three times before his companion said, "Maybe you should move along."

He looked puzzled but replied, "Good idea."

After the study he found out what he had actually said.

Then another pastor we know was asked a question in a leadership meeting. He meant to say, "Oh, well, that's easy to explain," but it came out as "Oh, hell, that's easy to explain."

Another pastor friend of ours was getting ready to perform a graveside funeral ceremony. It was a rainy day so a huge tarp was set over the grave and several times he directed people to the location by saying, "The wedding will take place over there." I always say pastors are in the "we marry'em, we bury 'em business" so sometimes the two can get confused.

One pastor gave a funeral service and instead of offering his condolences to the bereaved widow, he said, "Congratulations." Maybe he knew something the rest of us didn't know.

We heard of another minister who meant to say something was a "farce" and it came out as a bodily function that rhymes with dart. But that one is strictly hearsay.

Hell, I mean well, Zorro has had a few misspoken words over the years too. There was that time he used the word flatulent in a sermon a few times thinking it meant lazy. My daughter Shelly and I just kept looking at each other as if to say, "Did he say what I think he said?"

My favorite Zorro faux pax happened in Appalachia when he announced a church picnic. The park had a beautiful lake stocked full of fish so the planning committee decided to have a fishing contest. To ensure good participation, the committee asked Zorro to make the announcement and he agreed. He told everyone the time, place, and how the food would be served; then he meant to say, "We will all gather around the lake for your fishing pleasure..." However it came out, "Then we will all gather around the lake (he raised his hand at this point to give a big around type gesture for emphasis) for your pissing pleasure..." At first the congregation was silent. Soon you could hear the gradual swell of teeters here and there, then full blown laughter. Zorro realized what he said and got tickled.

Now let me explain what it is like when Zorro gets tickled. He cannot contain himself. Once in Washington he was reading a joke about a bricklayer during church services and he couldn't get through it because he kept bursting into laughter. The joke is about a guy who is explaining to the insurance company how he got injured by bricks because his foot got caught in a rope hooked to a wheel barrel of bricks and a scaffold. The joke is not that funny, but Zorro kept breaking up and doubling over in hysterics while he told it. I'm not sure if anyone ever got the gist of what he was saying. However, he and the congregation laughed so hard that it took a while for everyone to calm down.

Our custom was to record each church service for our tape library so people could check out sermons they missed or would like to hear again. We later found out this was the most checked out tape in the library. They had a long waiting list for people to get this tape. No one wanted to hear the sermon; they were having get-togethers just to hear Zorro trying to tell this joke.

When Zorro realized he had announced "pissing pleasure" instead of "fishing pleasure," he couldn't contain himself. He would catch a little composure then try to read the announcement again, but each time he reached the word "fishing" his voice got high and squeaky and he would lapse into giggles. The congregation would roar with laughter. Finally he just said, "You all come, you hear!" And they all did.

The Bible says laughter does a heart good, like medicine. Indeed it may be better than some medicine. Studies show laughter boosts your immune system, reduces stress, and increases blood flow. Laughter can also draw us closer to those around us. God created laughter and it is good!

To some, learning to laugh at ourselves may not be considered the weightier matters referred to in the Bible. On the other hand, I think it is definitely part of spiritual maturity or growth. We need to take our Christian calling, but not ourselves too seriously. Churches might be a little fuller if we laughed more and complained less.

When ministry can laugh at their faux pas and move on with life it endears them to those they are called to serve. Zorro and I have had much to laugh about over the years and we have learned that God can even use the word "unfitly" spoken to draw people into a closer relationship with him.

Zorro meant to say, "For your fishing pleasure..."

CHAPTER 17

UNAWARE ANGELS

"Be not forgetful to entertain strangers: for thereby some have entertained angels unawares."

—Hebrews 13:2 (KJV)

ZORRO AND I have done a lot of youth work through the years. Zorro is the one gifted with a certain rapport with the youth and I do a lot of behind the scenes organizing. That way I don't have to interface much with teenagers. I love the little darlings—just not as much as Zorro does.

One year we were returning late at night with a busload of teens from an activity in the Portland, Oregon, area. Zorro was driving the bus and I was following with a vanload of moms. We stopped about forty-five minutes outside of our destination, Tacoma, Washington, to gas up the vehicles and let the kids call their parents to pick them up at the church hall. The moms and I finished quickly and decided to head for home.

Zorro looked at me wryly. I knew what he was thinking. "My wife, who has no sense of direction, wants to go off on her own with five women on this foggy night. Should I say anything?" Being a wise husband, he wished me well and said he'd be there soon. However, with the fog and some snow residue left in the medians and on the side of the freeway, he did say, "Be careful!" Then he added, "And whatever you do, don't get a ticket!"

Men do not have much of a sense of humor when it comes to women with cars and tickets and such. Of course, the reason I couldn't get a ticket is because Zorro had a heavy foot in those days and already maxed us out ticket-wise. One more and our insurance would go up.

Did I mention it was Christmas Eve?

The ladies and I hopped in the van, eased onto the foggy freeway, and buzzed down the highway. Well, it didn't take too long for us to discover we were going the wrong direction. Don't ask me how all six of us missed the fact we got on the south freeway ramp instead of north. Unfortunately, the next exit was twenty-nine miles away with no rest areas or turn around spots in sight.

Suddenly, I thought, "There's snow in the median, but it's not deep. I bet I could just drive the van to the other side." Yes, it's against the law, but the other women thought it was a good idea, too. So I turned left and headed across the median. We reached the middle before the van got stuck. Then I learned a big life lesson: Just because there is snow on the ground, doesn't mean the ground is frozen. The ground could be thawed just enough to get your van stuck in the mud.

Now here I am with five chattering ladies stuck literally in the middle of nowhere. The only way to quiet them down was to say, "Let's pray!" No sooner had we said, "Amen!" when a car stopped on the north side, the direction we wished to go, and two men full of the Christmas spirit, if you know what I mean, hopped out and said, "Don't worry. We've called the police to help."

It is amazing how much can flash before your eyes in a split second. Visions similar to one of Dickens's ghosts in *A Christmas Carol* appeared hazily before my eyes. Yeah verily, it looked like Zorro, pointing a finger at me and spookily saying, "Whatever you do, don't get a ticket."

If the police came to help I would surely get a big, fat ticket.

The jolly men started walking toward the car. The women were concerned. I could tell because one said, "Lock the doors. I think we're going to die."

I sized up the situation, considered the stature and happy condition of the guys and figured three of us could sit on one and three on the other if they got frisky. Besides, had we not just prayed for rescue? I said, "These are our angels."

Visions of George Bailey in *It's a Wonderful Life* flashed in my mind. When he meets his angel Clarence for the first time, he heard his squeaky voice, looked at his polka-dot bow tie, and surveyed his stodgy demeanor. "Well," George said. "You look about the kind of angel I'd get. Sort of a fallen angel, aren't you? What happened to your wings?" That is about how I felt looking at my two inebriated angels.

In less than a wink, we were pushed out of the mud and onto pavement. We thanked the men profusely. They ran to their car, turned around and waved, saying, "Happy Christmas to all!"

Thoughts of Clement Moore's poem *A Visit from St. Nicholas* ran through my mind. Not to be out-quoted by a drunken angel, I yelled the next line. "And to all a good night!"

Our little adventure lasted less than ten minutes and my Christmas present was not receiving a police citation. When we arrived at the church right behind the bus, my husband said, "I thought you'd beat us here."

"Well, we took our time," I replied. I lifted my eyes to heaven and whispered, "Thank you, Lord." Then I thought about what Tiny Tim said in *A Christmas Carol.* "God bless us everyone!"

Merry Christmas!

CHAPTER 18

ITALIAN ADVENTURE

"When the time came, we set sail for Italy…"

—Acts 27:1 (NLT)

FOR OUR THIRTY-FIFTH wedding anniversary Zorro wanted to do something unforgettable. We had not traveled abroad much, so we decided a trip to Italy would be fun. Friends of ours had a daughter studying fashion design in Florence and wanted to visit her, so we combined efforts for the trip of a lifetime. There was no better way to celebrate than with our fun-loving *amici intimo* (Italian for close friends), Steve and Karon Smith.

We all wanted to save money and explore Italy on our own, so we arranged the trip ourselves. For almost a year we made preparations. It's amazing how inexpensively you can travel with a little forethought and planning. When the day came to board the plane for Italy, we were so excited we could hardly contain ourselves.

The Smith's daughter Tonya shared an apartment with two other fashion students in a quaint part of Florence in full view of the Arno River that cuts through the older part of the city. Florentines breathe great art and history, so they love their traditions and culture. We loved it, too. We saw the domed cathedral Duomo, the Medici Chapel, the Ufizzi Gallery, and the Academia where Michelangelo's David statue stands. We couldn't believe we were actually seeing masterpieces by great artists we had only read about.

We rented a car and did our own little tour of Tuscany, saw the leaning Tower of Pisa, gazed at the Mediterranean Sea, and slept at a bed and breakfast in Lucca, whose Renaissance era walls surrounding the city are still intact. Lucca was the only place we had a substandard meal. Maybe the cooks thought they were still in the Renaissance era. The food everywhere else, even little out of the way places, was a gourmet delight. The pastas were light and fluffy. The pizza crust all handmade. I loved the bruschetta, gelato, and Italian ice. This was Italian food like you've never eaten before.

We turned in our car because the rest of our itinerary would be easily accessible by train. Venice was our next stop. I thought Venice was the most romantic city in the world. Of course, I haven't seen the world, but I loved the Doge's Palace, Saint Mark's Basilica, and those gondola rides through the waterway streets in Venice.

At Piazza San Marco, the huge square considered the gathering place for Venice, you could feed the pigeons, sip house wine at outdoor cafes, and listen to live music while gazing at landmarks like the palace, cathedral, and Grand Canal. Of course, feeding those pigeons reminded me of a scene from Alfred Hitchcock's *The Birds*. What did it matter? We were in Venice! It didn't matter that our room was the size of a thimble; we were in Venice! Actually, our room was the size of a thimble. It was so small that one of us had

Zorro and me in front with Steve and Karon in back: We
loved those gondola rides in Venice!

to stand or lay on the bed so the other one could pass by.
But what did it matter? We were in Venice!

From Venice we took the train to Rome where we
checked into a lovely hotel with huge rooms Steve found
through the Internet for a fantastic price. It seems God
saved our best accommodation for last. The room was so
large Zorro and I could walk around the room side-by-side
at the same time. We even had a bath tub and a bidet. Most
places we stayed we were lucky if we had a shower stall.
First thing I did in Rome was take a bubble bath.

We had been instructed to hold on carefully to our passports because pickpocketing is a major industry in Rome.
We could either leave them with the hotel desk clerk to

retrieve when we checked out, or keep them in the small safe in our room. We opted to leave them at the desk. My passport picture was the best I'd ever taken. Usually they look like grumpy mug shots, but in this one I was smiling and looked ten years younger.

We visited the Pantheon, Piazza Navona, the Arch of Constantine, Palatine Hill, and the Spanish steps. As cheap as we are, we actually paid for tours of the Colosseum, the Forum, Vatican City, St. Peter's Basilica, and the Sistine Chapel. It was money well spent because we would have overlooked a lot of history, artwork, and architecture without a guide. We wanted to see as much as possible. Even though we tossed our coins in the Trevi Fountain, we weren't sure it would guarantee us a return trip to Rome like the legend suggests.

Zorro and me tossing coins over our shoulders
into the Trevi Fountain

On the last day of our trip, we decided to split up. Steve and Karon had plans. Zorro found out it was a day the pope was supposed to make an appearance at Vatican City so he wanted to go take a "peek at the pope." I decided to do a little shopping instead. We would all meet back at the hotel for dinner and packing. Tomorrow we would be saying, "Arrivederci, Roma!"

It was getting late and Zorro still hadn't returned from taking a "peek at the pope." I wasn't too concerned because Zorro sometimes loses track of time. Finally, he came in the room and said, "You will never believe what happened!" Uh-oh I thought. I don't like the sound of this. He continued with, "I've been robbed!"

When Zorro returned from Vatican City he boarded a bus packed like sardines. A boy not more than ten years old grabbed the rear door handles and violently jostled the crowded passengers with his chest. Quickly his two young accomplices emptied the pockets of the unsuspecting passengers while their attention was diverted by yelling at the young boy creating the disturbance. Zorro then realized his passport pouch with credit cards and cash strapped "securely" under his shirt for safekeeping was gone. Gripped with disbelief and terror, he confronted the kids who immediately offered to help by checking the pockets of everyone else as they lifted their wallets, too. Then they disappeared in an escape car waiting at the next bus stop. To make matters worse, the pope didn't even make his appearance that day.

I asked the usual questions. "Are you all right? How much did they get? Do we need to cancel our credit cards?" Then I said, "Thank God they didn't get our passports!"

"Um-er-ah-well," Zorro stammered. "Well, you see, I decided to pick up our passports today instead of tomorrow when we check out. I was going to put them in the safe but I forgot. Um-er-ah-well they got the passports, too."

Up until then I had been pretty sympathetic. We had both agreed we would not carry our passports around town just in case something like this happened. I was not pleased.

It wouldn't have been so bad if we weren't leaving the next day because I had photocopies of our passports, driver's licenses, and credit cards. However, trying to get passports replaced in the morning and getting to the airport in time to catch our plane could be a problem. We just prayed about it and left it in God's hands. If it was his will, we'd make the plane.

When we went to the police station to file a report, we discovered a long line of people who had also been robbed. The Italian police took their sweet time processing everyone. After all, it's not like they don't deal with this every day. No way any of us would ever see our passports, money, or credit cards again.

Then we found a little photo shop still open to take our replacement passport pictures. Needless to say, this picture of me was not quite as flattering as the last one. It looked like a grumpy mug shot. We packed and planned to wait with our photocopied documents and new passport pictures at the United States Consulate fence when they opened at nine in the morning.

The next day we bid farewell to our amici intimo and said, "We shall see you when we see you," hopped in a taxi and headed for the consulate. The woman who assisted us was helpful and efficient. As she issued us temporary passports she told us not to be embarrassed. Pickpocketing is one of Italy's national pastimes and almost an art form to some thieves. She had even replaced passports for sheriffs, FBI agents, undercover police officers, and secret service men. One woman had her wallet stolen from inside her purse while standing in a subway car clutching the zipped purse in both her hands in front of her.

With our new passports in hand we rushed to the airport. Our plane had just loaded and we had ten minutes before it was scheduled to take off. We needed to scurry through our check points to make our flight. I love Italians, but they do not hurry to accommodate anyone. Even though our plane remained sitting there for another hour, we were not allowed to board. We were told, "It is assolutamente impossibile!"

So off the Smiths flew while we pondered our next option. Evidently, it was not God's will for us to leave Italy on that flight. We always pray for God's will to be done in our lives, but most of the time we pray it thinking his will is ours. God does not hop at our every request and life is full of glitches. So now we had two choices: we could fuss and fume over being left behind or just laugh it off and go with the flow. Were we going to let this inconvenience taint the wonderful time we had in Italy? No way!

Top priority was to rebook our flight so we rushed to the American Airlines counter. Although it was "American" Airlines only one lone, young Italian man was working. One couple was ahead of us at the counter, but soon a line began to form behind us. The young Italian man was extremely slow. He sluggishly typed info into the computer with his two index fingers using the old hunt and peck method. It took over an hour to process the couple in front of us. We were not encouraged when we heard someone behind us reply, "Yea, I remember a couple of years ago when I missed a flight. It took me a week to get out of Rome."

Judging by the speed of this employee, that was not unbelievable. Another man said, "You're in Italy now. I hope you like it here. You may be here a long time."

Well I did like Italy, but I really wanted to go home. Finally our turn came. It took him a long time to book us on the next flight out, which was tomorrow at the same time. Praise God we got those tickets. We definitely were not going to complain because after he finished with us, he closed for the day. Everyone else in line had to come back tomorrow.

We decided to stay at the airport hotel so we would be sure not to miss our plane. We checked in, relaxed, drank some wine, ate a nice meal, and watched some Italian TV. You know what they say, "When in Rome, do as the Romans do!"

Zorro almost had a heart attack when he figured out the missed flight, new passports, and extra night in Rome cost more than a thousand dollars. Well, he wanted a memorable trip. This was definitely one anniversary Zorro would never forget.

Zorro and me at an outdoor café in Rome: Not even having our passports stolen and missing our flight home would ruin our Roman holiday!

CHAPTER 19

GIFTS FROM GOD

"Children are a blessing and a gift from the Lord."

—Psalm 127:3
(Contemporary English Version)

WHEN OUR GRANDDAUGHTER Sophia was born, I was privileged to witness her birth. It's the first time I had ever seen a baby actually being born and I can tell you, it is not a pretty sight.

When the head crowns, it is not all round and smooth like you see in the movies. It's bumpy and a little distorted, looking more like an alien than a human. This is understandable since the baby is straining to push out a tiny opening that logically it should not be able to get through. As my mother used to say, "It's like pulling a doorknob through a keyhole."

My daughter Shelly opted not to take drugs so she could experience the euphoria and beauty of childbirth.

As baby Sophia made her grand appearance, our usually reserved Shelly let out a scream to rival those you hear in horror movies.

A mother in a nearby birthing room told a nurse, "Oh, I hear the baby cry."

The nurse replied, "No, dear. That's the mother."

Baby Sophia looked a little bluish purple and was none too happy as they put her on Shelly's tummy. Daddy Dale was there to cut the cord and presto/chango right before my very eyes she turned pink and plump, all eight pounds, nine ounces of her. By the time she was weighed, swaddled, and placed at her mommy's breast, Sophia had transformed from your average alien-looking baby into an angelic, newborn babe. This was quite a metamorphosis.

I must admit I've always been fascinated by the whole pregnancy and child birth process. Thoughts of Shelly's birth, our firstborn, resurfaced. In those days, knowing the sex of the child was not an option. When Shelly was born my husband was in a better position to assess everything so I excitedly asked him, "What is it?"

In his awe of the miracle of birth he just kept saying, "It's a baby! It's a baby!"

I thought, "Thank God. I would have hated to go to all this trouble for a monkey."

Shelly and our second daughter Sherisa were born nineteen months apart and the births were very similar. Both were girls, were born on the same day of the month (10th), at the exact same time of day (7:45 a.m.), weighed the same (9 pounds), were the same length (21 inches), delivered by the same midwife, and at the same place. However that is where the similarities end because they definitely have their own personalities and are opposites on most everything else.

Matthew came ten years later. No, he wasn't a surprise. Our daughters were preteens, which is such a cute age that

Zorro and I woke up one morning and said, "Let's have another one."

I call it Planned Parenthood—poor planning because of the age difference between him and the girls, but it all works out. If we had waited until the girls were teens I'm sure we would have thought longer and harder, but probably would have made the same decision.

Matthew's birth was not in any way like our girls' births. He was born in a motel room while we were traveling. It wasn't a "no room at the inn" scenario like in the Bible, but just one of those things. Babies come when they are ready, not according to a timetable. Although inconvenient, we were thankful he was healthy and happy. As he grew we discovered we had three opposites, if such a thing was possible.

Baby Matthew's surprise arrival in a motel room didn't keep us from celebrating. Shelly, Zorro, Sherisa and even baby Matthew enjoy a chocolate cigar.

Having gone through childbirth three times, I can think of no other experience that has reinforced the existence of God to me as much as feeling life inside my body and bringing a baby into the world. I wonder how anyone can think such a miracle is the product of evolution.

There are many arguments in today's society for not having children. Movies make babies look all cute and cuddly, but the first few months can be grueling. Endless diaper changes, feedings, and sleepless nights take a lot of emotional and physical energy, which can intensify if a baby has health problems or the colic. Children change marriage dynamics. Priorities rearrange as spouses defer to the inconvenience of a helpless infant. Free time becomes a thing of the past.

As children grow, parents realize what a huge commitment and responsibility they are. Children do not make for an orderly lifestyle. They're messy. They make mistakes. Parents make mistakes. It costs a lot of money to raise a child. It also takes a lot of hard work, energy, and time. Parents try various methods to communicate, educate, teach, and impart spiritual and moral values. They worry about them and hurt for them. Parents struggle watching children make choices they wouldn't make—not always wrong choices, but different because they are not little robot versions of us. Parents wrestle with how tightly to hold on, how soon to let go.

These are valid arguments for not bringing a child into an overpopulated, evil world. In biblical times children were considered a blessing. Today they are considered an inconvenience. However, many worthwhile things are inconvenient such as marriage, family, church, friends, and anything to do with people. Babies are no exception, so I can understand why people choose not to have or adopt children.

Yet, for me, I think God used my children to teach me some of the most valuable lessons of life. If I have any of the fruits of God's Holy Spirit it's probably because of Shelly, Sherisa, and Matthew. My little alien babies turned pretty and pink. In spite of the sleepless nights, I thought every sigh, smile, laugh, and move they made was adorable. They opened my eyes to the creation around me by forcing me to look at sunsets, butterflies, trees, bugs, and flowers. I learned to cope with worry, doubt, frustration, and the realization that my way wasn't always the best for them. I shared their joy and shared their pain. I found out there was something more important in the universe than me. I learned to "let go and let God!"

The miracle of children amazes me, even more when I think of God referring to us as his children. Do I really comprehend what a bountiful blessing it is to be called a child of God? It means God is willing to care for me in spite of how messy and inconvenient I am. He loves me with a deeper love than I could ever imagine bestowing on my own children or grandchildren. And that, my friend, is a lot of love!

Shelly, Matthew, and Sherisa: Our three little blessings are big blessings now that they are all grown up!

CHAPTER 20

TIME TO PARTY

"*The next day Jesus' mother was a guest at a wedding celebration in the village of Cana in Galilee... The wine supply ran out during the festivities, so Jesus' mother spoke to him about the problem.*

'They have no more wine,' she told him... his mother told the servants, 'Do whatever he tells you.'... Jesus told the servants, 'Fill the jars with water.... Dip some out and take it to the master of ceremonies.'

So they followed his instructions. When the master of ceremonies tasted the water that was now wine... he said... 'you have kept the best until now!' This miraculous sign at Cana in Galilee was Jesus' first display of his glory."

—John 2:1-11 (NLT)

OUR DAUGHTERS EACH had beautiful weddings and they both know how to throw a party.

In September 2000 our oldest daughter Shelly married Dale Davis on the island of Maui in a little chapel overlooking the beach. A luau reception followed at a cabana and we partied on a moonlit beach while we watched Hawaiian dancers entertain us, feasted on delicacies, drank champagne, and did the hula under the stars to live music until the wee hours of the morning.

Our daughter Sherisa married Randy Emata in a very traditional-eclectic wedding (if such a thing is possible) at a large church in San Jose, California in April 1999. Her dad walked her down the aisle to the live accompaniment of a four-string quartet and amidst the traditional fare her best friend Eileen did an interpretive dance, I sang a song I wrote entitled *A Mother's Prayer*, and the families came forward to unite in prayer.

Randy and Sherisa thought it would be fun to forego the usual wedding march and as a surprise to her grandfather (my dad) stroll out to his favorite song. Randy is a professional musician so he arranged for some friends and family in the congregation to bring instruments. One by one they rose at the end of the ceremony and started playing a Dixieland version of *When the Saints Go Marching In*. Down the center aisle the band marched and the rest of us just danced out the door following Randy and Sherisa's lead. My elderly dad smiled and said, "I love that song," as he boogied out the door.

Both girls insisted their brother Matthew, who is ten years younger, stand on their side of the wedding party along with their bride's maids. Matthew loved it. For years he said, "Always a bride's maid, never a bride." That's funny when you live as close to San Francisco as we do.

Matthew, Shelly, and Sherisa at Sherisa's wedding

Both weddings were performed by their dad. You know him as Zorro.

On Randy and Sherisa's tenth anniversary we received an invitation to their vow renewal party in "retro, wild and crazy Old Downtown Las Vegas" with a 50s/60s theme. They wanted no presents but requested everyone come in costumes representative of the era. The festivities took place in a private atrium at the Golden Nugget.

Sherisa asked her dad to dress as Zorro. Since Zorro® was a popular TV show from that time, we thought it would be appropriate. However, the real reason she wanted him dressed that way is because all these Zorro stories are a part of her life and have special meaning to her. She even sent all those invited the story about how Zorro got his name.

To tell the truth I wasn't excited about parading around Vegas in costume, but I had to. Party time awaited! Besides, we just needed to get from the car to the private room. Zorro looked pretty good all decked out with his mask, cape and sword. I went as a senorita, Mrs. Zorro. My black wig looked more like Elvira, Mistress of the Dark (the woman who used to introduce the late-night horror flicks on TV) than Catherine Zeta Jones from the Zorro® movie, but at least I had a Spanish fan to cover my face when needed.

As we boarded the elevator in the parking garage, people asked, "Going to a costume party?" Zorro grinned, winked and said, "We dress like this every Saturday night." I must admit Zorro caused quite a stir just walking through the halls at the Golden Nugget. People stared and whispered, "There's Zorro." Some even wanted to have pictures taken with him. So many wanted pictures taken with Zorro that he's thought about dressing up, going back, and charging a fee to supplement our income when he eventually retires.

The private atrium wasn't quite as private as we hoped. Red ropes, like those used for VIPs, separated us off from the public, but we were still in full view of everyone passing by. We attracted a lot of attention. And why not? We certainly had our share of VIPs. Sherisa and Randy were Marilyn Monroe and Elvis. We had Dean Martin, Frank Sinatra, JFK, Jacqueline Kennedy, Danny Zucho, James Dean, pony-tailed gals, nerdy guys, some show girls, flower children, and even Dorothy with Toto from the *Wizard of Oz*. I know Dorothy's from a different era but no one in costume was turned away. We were starting to feel like celebrities as we gained quite a crowd of onlookers. One bellowed, "Hey, Zorro," and gave us two thumbs up.

So with Vegas gazing on we ate a sumptuous dinner interspersed with Mr. and Mrs. Z sharing impromptu advice for a long and happy marriage: praise one another, cultivate, don't dominate, give your mate freedom to be themselves, say, "Yes, dear" a lot, and remember that a successful marriage means falling in love over and over again—always with the same person. Others shared advice as well. Some shared what they admired about Sherisa and Randy.

Zorro did the vow renewal. Our son Matthew and our grandson Dakota gave touching tributes and toasts. Elvis and Marilyn exchanged huge, gaudy but tasteful rings and took a few promenades around the room while we all sang "ta-da-de-da" to the tune of *Here Comes the Bride*. On one such romp around the room a man at the red rope said to Sherisa, "What's the occasion, Marilyn?"

She replied, "It's our tenth wedding anniversary."

The guy said, "If you need anything, please let me know. I'm the owner."

Sherisa smiled and thought, "Yeah, right."

However, when she sat down at the table the waitress said, "Oh, I didn't know you were friends of the owner."

The staff had already been very accommodating, but now treated us even better. They seemed to really respond to the costumed theme with "Can I get you anything else, King?" or "Can I freshen that drink for you, Marilyn?"

The party continued at an upstairs lounge where we again had a special red roped off area usually reserved for VIPs. We danced into the wee hours of the morning. Many Golden Nugget patrons had their pictures taken with Marilyn Monroe, Elvis, and Zorro. What a night! I think God was smiling.

Sometimes we put God in a box and say, "Oh, he wouldn't approve." I think God laughs with us and parties with us. Of course God is not pleased with drunkenness, lewdness, or vulgarity, but we can party and have a good time without those elements. Sometimes we mistake sanctimony for godliness. God loves to laugh with us. Why not invite him to the party?

I delight thinking about Jesus' first miracle, when he turned water into wine at the wedding party. Some feel if God walked into a room they would need to tone it down a bit. I think, "Hey, God's here! Time to party!" When my kids think of God I want them to see him there with them at the party, having a good time.

Zorro and me in Vegas: We know that God loves to laugh. If you let him, he will laugh with you. If you don't, he'll laugh at you. We'd rather be laughing with God.